COOPERATING
WITH YOUR
DESTINY

DISCOVERING GOD'S
PLAN FOR YOUR LIFE

DR. ED KING

Melbourne, Florida USA

Cooperating With Your Destiny—Discovering God's Plan for Your Life
by Ed King

Parsons Publishing House
P. O. Box 410063
Melbourne, FL 32940 USA
www.ParsonsPublishingHouse.com
Info@ParsonsPublishingHouse.com

TABLE OF CONTENTS

INTRODUCTION

> "For I know the plans I have for you," declares
> the LORD, "plans to prosper you and not to
> harm you, plans to give you hope and a future"
> (Jeremiah 29:11, NIV).

What is my purpose in life? Is there a reason that I am alive? What is my destiny? Have you ever pondered these questions? While these are often common considerations, the truth is, God had a purpose for your life conceived before you were ever born. This plan that God has laid out for you is unique and meant perfectly for you. Your destiny was orchestrated before the very foundation of the world. It is a good plan that will bring you fulfillment, peace, and joy—more than you could ever imagine!

> You saw me before I was born. Every day of my
> life was recorded in your book. Every moment
> was laid out before a single day had passed
> (Psalm 139:16, NLT).

Destiny requires a blending of God's plan and our cooperation. As God works His plan, and we make a decision to follow Him, destiny is fulfilled. Pursuing destiny requires relationship, and ultimately, a partnership with God. To truly walk in your destiny from God, you must pursue relationship with Him and daily work together in harmony.

While God has designed your destiny, the responsibility to fulfill it is yours. Your purpose will not be fulfilled passively; action on your behalf is required. Cooperating with God's plan entails walking in it and fulfilling it in a joint effort with God. Similarly, you are not called to simply pursue the will of God, you are called to finish the will of God. We are called to discover God's plan and, ultimately, to use what we have been given with perseverance. Run the race that God has set before you, and with Him by your side, you will not fail!

> And we know that in all things God works for the good of those who love him, who have been called according to his purpose (Romans 8:28, NLT).

You can step out in confidence knowing that God's plan and desire is to prosper those things to which you apply yourself and to bless your life! As you cooperate within your God-given destiny, He will bring all of heaven's resources to your access under His mighty provision and care. God will lead you down a path of success and fulfillment as you follow Him. It will not always be easy because there is an enemy, the devil! However, it will always be worth it as God guides you in a perfectly orchestrated, purposeful journey.

Your obedience to step out in faith is all that is needed to start this adventure! Dive into your destiny and watch God move on your behalf!

1

DESTINED BY GOD

The concept of destiny is often misunderstood, but it is undoubtedly worth talking about because God thought it important enough to address the subject. Scripture tells us that God had a plan for us from before the foundation of the world. This plan was, and is, well-constructed—well-thought-out in the mind of God long before we were ever conceived and born into the world.

In the Bible, you can find references to the term "predestine" or "predestinate." The word "destiny" is a synonym or derivative of the word "destination." You get an idea of destiny because you have a destination, and you are going somewhere.

When you go on a trip of any distance, you may use a GPS (global positioning system) in your car, phone, tablet, or even your wristwatch to arrive at your destination successfully. After you enter the destination, the GPS will direct you to the front door of where you want to go. Inside the GPS, there is software that plans your route, which is significant in and of itself. However, we have another and greater GPS working for us, a *God Positioning System*, and there is a plan that He has put in motion for our lives.

Sometimes, we think that because God has a destiny for us, that it will automatically happen. We believe that all we need to do is show up, and we're done. When we see the word "predestined," we get the idea that we cannot alter or change things, and we are stuck with it regardless of what happens. However, that idea is not even close to correct and definitely not a biblical truth.

DESTINY FROM PSALMS

Let's talk about our destiny from the book of Psalms:

> The Lord is the portion of mine inheritance
> and of my cup: thou maintainest my lot. The
> lines are fallen unto me in pleasant places; yea,
> I have a goodly heritage (Psalm 16:5-6).

There are six words I want to emphasize in that passage that has to do with your destiny. These words tell us a great deal about how things work in God's Kingdom; the words are *portion, inheritance, cup, lot, lines,* and *heritage.*

When you think about these six words, they all originate from God's side of the spiritual realm—none of which you control. You do not control your portion, inheritance, cup, or lot. Also beyond your control are the lines and heritage. There is nothing you can do to change any of them because they are all divinely given, inspired, and granted. Therefore, they have the seal of destiny on them. These are compelling words that I want to define so we have a better understanding.

The first word is **portion** and is defined as something weighed out. Having a part or portion is like going to the grocery store and picking out five apples and four cucumbers. You have taken only a few pieces, a very small part of a much larger amount in the bin. It was a portion—something that was weighed out. It was a ration or a part of a larger whole.

God has an exclusive portion in life reserved for you—He gives a good portion and good plan to everyone. None of us will come up short or be disappointed with what He intends for us, but remember: your portion is not mine, and mine is not yours.

The word **"inheritance"** refers to an allotment. We know that we are joint-heirs with Christ, which includes an inheritance. But, we also have a specific and unique inheritance that is ours alone. Please understand that we have a generic word from God that comes to all of us, found in the Bible; in addition, God gives personal words to us individually. You are distinctly gifted. You were born in a specific area, arena, and time, and you were raised by a particular set of parents. All these things contribute to making you uniquely who and what you are.

The next word is **cup** and is often found in the Bible. Scripture talks about our cup running over, with the cup being our provision or blessing. There is the cup of blessing and the communion cup. There are many times that the Lord uses "cup" when He talks about an outpouring. In Psalm 23, He said my cup overflows, and goodness and mercy follow it. There is something about the cup that is unique and special.

Then He talks about the word "lot," but we will come back to that one later.

The word **"line"** is defined as a cord or a rope, which again means a portion, but in this case it indicates something that restrains us. A good illustration of "line" would be a leash on a

3

dog. If you have a long retractable leash, then your dog has a little more running room. Conversely, if you have a short leash, the dog is more restrained and is not going far. There is a line that lets that animal move only so far from a central location. This is the way that "line" works; it is talking about a boundary.

The next word is **heritage**, which is synonymous with inheritance or estate; it means to distribute, bequeath, or that which is given. You earn none of that by working for it; it is a gift. A person receiving an inheritance has no control over what or how much it is or to whom it is given. The giver of the inheritance—in this case, God—solely arranges the disbursement.

All these terms hinge on the word "lot," which carries with it the idea of portion; however, it is more accurately defined as **destiny**.

YOUR LOT IN LIFE

"**Lot**" can also indicate a piece of real estate. When you build a house, you put it on a lot with boundaries that define the property regardless of the size. If you decide to build on another person's lot, you are going to get into trouble. That is why boundaries are there. You must stay inside your borders, just as your neighbors must stay inside theirs.

You might use the term "lot" by saying, "This is my lot in life." It is something that is determined by others over which you have no control; you have no choice but to walk in it. No matter how strong your desire, you cannot control your destiny because it is given to you by God.

As mentioned earlier, think about the word "lot" as a real estate term. Imagine that you are going to build a house, and your first step is to search for a piece of real estate—a lot to put it on. You may visit a new housing development where homes are in the beginning stages of planning and building, and you look at all the available lots. You will find there are many different lot sizes and configurations, with varied views, road frontages, and backyards.

You choose a lot based on the style of house you want and where you want it built—evaluating many factors. In this scenario, a "lot" is a building term. Typically, the bigger the lot, the more it will cost. You choose your lot based on what you want and how much you are willing to invest; however, the lot we are discussing in this chapter is not chosen by you.

Each real estate lot has containments or boundaries. Once you get your parameters set and realize your lot is 200 feet by 200 feet, it establishes boundaries that are called "lines." Just like the dog on the leash we mentioned earlier, the lot determines the line. The lot determines how big the boundaries are.

The Bible says, "Enlarge the place of thy tent, and let them stretch forth the curtains of thine habitations: spare not, lengthen thy cords, and strengthen thy stakes" (Isaiah 54:2). This verse means to pull the tent pegs out of the ground and stretch them out for the purpose of enlargement. In other words, there are certain times when stretching the boundaries must happen.

Included in this lot given by God is a containment. You contain—you have the parameters and all the things that are related to the lot. There is an inheritance that is given to us by God, and it is not merely something we choose.

These six words mentioned in Psalm 16 have to do with your destiny. They have to do with something we cannot do on our own. These things are something we move toward but not something we control.

I heard a good illustration of destiny the other day. If I'm on level ground, I might be able to take my car out of gear and push it until it moves a little bit. However, no matter how hard I try, I can't move it very far and definitely not uphill—it weighs too much and has more power than I have strength. However, I can get in the car, start it up, and cooperate with what makes it run. By sheer force, you cannot make it do what it is supposed to do; you don't have enough power to do it. That is the way the destiny of God works in your life. You do not control or run it. You do not choose it; you only cooperate with it.

Boundary Lines

Let's look in Jeremiah:

> For I know the plans I have for you declares the Lord, plans to prosper you and not to harm you, plans to give you hope and a future (Jeremiah 29:11, NIV).

This verse covers everything contained on that lot which God has destined for you. According to God, that plan, plot, or lot is to prosper you and give you hope and a future. When you get into your destiny, lot, plan, or purpose of God, it will not harm you; it will not kill or destroy you. In fact, it will bless you and prosper your life. It will give you the right kind of future.

This verse could be translated as God has a plan to give you a hope and a destiny. The word "destiny" is appropriate here. God has an incredible and unique plan for each one of us. When I say "unique," I mean that your lot in life is quite different from my lot. Your lot creates different boundaries than mine—not necessarily better or worse, just different.

All of us must live life by boundaries and limits. God gives us a lot of running room between those limits, but trouble awaits if you stray beyond them. Those boundaries are the Word of God, the law of God, the ways of God, and the purposes of God. We could say it is the Ten Commandments, but it is broader than that. In the New Testament, the Ten Commandments have been summed up in the one perfect law of love; we have an eleventh commandment that incorporates all the others. God gives us limits for life, and all of us must live by them. There is no question or debate; everyone has the same limitations.

However, there is a uniqueness to you and a uniqueness to me, not a crossover. For example: when the children of Israel came into the Promised Land, and the tribes received their land and inheritance, which was their lot given to them. It sounded something like this:

> *Everything is yours from that mountain to the north, to the river to its right, to those hills beyond, to the sea in the distance and that large rock formation to its south. But, beyond that rock and beyond that mountain, that is someone else's.*

All of us live under a universal law, but with a different lot. Everyone has a lot in life.

Your eyes saw my unformed substance, and in
Your book all the days [of my life] were written
before ever they took shape, when as yet there
was none of them (Psalm 139:16, AMPC).

In other words, God knew everything about you, even before
you were conceived. I believe that without question.

God has a plan for your life conceived before you were born. It
is a good plan that will not harm you and will have a good
outcome. It has a good end. However, that does not mean that
it is always easily obtainable. You will not be rewarded when
you get to heaven for how easy it was. There are things you will
need to overcome in this life, which is just part of being here.
You must be an overcomer to walk in the destiny God has for
you.

2
WALKING AFTER TRUTH

There are two schools of thought that come to mind when discussing destiny. The first is that God controls your destiny, and there is nothing you can do about it. You have no choice or sanction; your destiny is all prearranged and predetermined. *"Que Será Será;* whatever will be, will be." You just wake up each morning, and it automatically happens, and there is nothing anyone can do about it. If God wants it to happen, it will, but if God does not want it to happen, it won't. Some people actually approach life that way.

Then there is the other thought: "I control my own destiny." You hear that a lot regarding athletic teams—especially around the playoffs and postseason. The color commentator says, *"Well, Jim, in my opinion, in the Southeastern Conference, LSU and Alabama control their own destiny."* The problem is that the statement is incorrect; they do not control it because there are many factors at play. The star quarterback could be injured? Something tragic could happen to one or more of their best players. As you can see, they do not control their destiny.

This ideology of controlling your own destiny is cheaply used by many people in our culture, and not just in the sports arena. It is one of those statements that permeates through society in almost everything we do.

Even in the church, we begin to buy into the fact that we control our destiny. However, like in our sports illustration, you do not. Think back to those six terms from Psalms that we covered in chapter one. The lot, the line, and the heritage all come from God's side. God is the provider of the cup—not you. You do not do any of that; God does it.

DESTINY'S TRUTH IS IN THE MIDDLE

There are two ways that we approach destiny: God controls it all, and there is nothing we can do about it, or we control it all, and everything is in our hands. Yet, neither thought is 100% correct; the truth is that destiny is a combination of the two.

Destiny involves a mixture of God's ability and our cooperation. It is God's knowledge of the future and His understanding of how you were made. It is God who put things in you that He wants in there, but we must cooperate with those things.

There are many things about your life that you did not choose or have any control over. Yes, you do have control over what you do with what has been given to you, but absolutely no determination over what you were given in the first place. You did not choose your lot, nor the size of it.

Destiny is a combination of God working His plan and our decision to cooperate with that plan. Destiny requires partnership. To walk in the destiny of God, you must become His partner and work closely with Him. You can't just go off somewhere and do your own thing. You need to do what God wants.

Cooperating with God's Plan

We need to find God's plan and work with it. There is a phrase often used to motivate young people just starting out in life. It sounds something like: *"With enough hard work, you can be anything you want to be."* It sounds good, but at face value, that statement is inaccurate. The truth is that you can only be anything you want to be if it fits on your lot.

You have been given a lot that is particularly suited to you. Without much consideration, you might say, *"But, I want to be on that lot over there. I think I'd like it better."* I'm so sorry, but you can't be on that lot; it's not yours. One of the things required for cooperating with God's destiny is understanding who you are and being happy with it. However, if you discover that you just can't comply, you can forget about walking in the destiny of God. You need to know who you are and start liking what God made.

> ## You can only be anything you want to be **if** it fits on your lot.

Start liking and accepting yourself so that you will be able to fulfill the plan that God has for your life down the road. Some might say, *"But I really don't like me very much, and I want to be someone else."* Sorry, but you are not someone else. In fact, you will still be you—and no one else—in six months, ten years, or fifty-million years from today. You will be you forever, so you might as well start liking and accepting yourself so that you will be able to fulfill the plan that God has for your life.

Destiny is a combination of God working on your behalf—doing what you cannot do—while you cooperate with Him in the process. A partnership suggests both are needed and required. We must find God's plan, and in our best interest, work closely with it.

Let's look again at Psalm 16:

> The Lord is the portion of mine inheritance
> and of my cup: thou maintainest my lot. The
> lines are fallen unto me in pleasant places; yea,
> I have a goodly heritage (Psalm 16:5-6).

Again, these words—portion, inheritance, cup, lot, line, and heritage—are controlled and distributed by the Lord. We have no control over them at all.

A lot is a piece of ground that we build on. Our lot establishes our boundary lines. This Bible passage shows how things are connected. Everything radiates from the lot.

GAMBLING WITH OUR FUTURE

When someone gambles, they are casting lots. For example, people may draw straws, where drawing the short straw involves certain undesirable events coming your way. You may have to be the designated driver on a long trip or pay the green fees for your golfing buddies, or you may have to wear a clown suit to dinner. Conversely, if you draw the long straw, something good will happen for you.

As a young man, I gambled a time or two, but I have never been a gambler. People throw dice, play poker, and many other games of chance. Even the Roman soldiers cast lots of some kind for the robe of Jesus.

There is not much in Scripture concerning gambling, but many people have a great deal to say about it. Gambling may be frowned upon in certain circles because of casting lots in the Bible, but there is no verse that I know of that says, *"Thou shalt not gamble."*

The lottery, which has its roots in the word "lot," is one of the most popular forms of gambling in our society. The whole concept of the lottery is a huge game of chance. People hope they can win it and get all their cups running over, boundaries stretched, and their inheritance without partnering with God.

The Lord has told you what He would give you if you partnered with Him, but some want to get the lot without the partnership. This happens when someone tries to establish their own destiny.

Many people want the lot without the partnership with God.

There are countless stories of people who win extreme amounts of money by playing the lottery. I read a story about a person who won $300 million, but they were completely broke within five years. That is an example of trying to get the inheritance without it being given to you by the One who holds your future.

When we take our life into our own hands, we are trying to formulate our destiny without listening to God's plan. There is no difference between that and playing the lottery. In essence, we are saying, *"I don't need You, God. I'll tell You when You can get involved, but I don't need You right now. Don't bother me because I've got it all figured out."* We are telling God that we know more about our lives than He does. We don't want His dream, His vision, His plan, or His purpose. We don't want anything He's laying out for us because we want to run our own life.

If we try to take our lives into our hands, it is the equivalent to rolling dice for our future. I hope your career and everything in your life works out! When we fail to cooperate with the destiny of God, everything will be judged because we failed to submit our life to God.

LIVING OUT YOUR PORTION

A lot in life is something given to a person by divine providence; it is our portion in life. Some look and think they want another's lot, and they try to emulate them because they want a different portion. You may say, *"I want to do what they do. I want to be like them."* We want that rather than finding out what God wants and has for us.

When the children of Israel came into the Promised Land, they were given a portion of it for all eternity. It was not temporary or given to them for only a season. It was theirs, but they had to possess it. There were giants and all kinds of enemies that tried to take their land. In fact, Israel's enemies are still trying to take it today! They had to possess it, but it was theirs. God gave it to them—forever.

The land of Israel would not prosper with any other people on it. In the same way, if someone tries to get on your lot, it will not prosper them, either. You will find that it will not work for you if you attempt to live on someone else's lot.

Playing the lottery with life is living our lives for a destiny that we choose for ourselves—playing the lottery with our eternity.

14

God has already promised us what He would do in our lives, but we must choose to cooperate with it.

Let's go back and read Psalm 16:

> "The Lord is the portion of mine inheritance
> and of my cup: thou maintainest my lot.The
> lines are fallen unto me in pleasant places; yea,
> I have a goodly heritage" (Psalm 16:5-6).

God said that when we stay on our lot—accepting the lot He gives us—the lines or the boundaries of our lives fall in pleasant places. In other words, you will be pleased with the life that God gives you if you cooperate with it. Conversely, you will not like the one you get if you abandon His plan. The plan that you create will not be filled with pleasant places. You will reap the destruction of the whirlwind.

King Saul was given a "lot" or a destiny in God, and we see what miserable results he derived from making his own choices. He ended up going to a witch to discover his future rather than to the One qualified to bring about his lot. He wanted a different lot than the one he had. After King Saul sought his future through the medium—a witch—his life completely fell apart. At that point, he started rolling the dice on his future rather than listening to the mind of the Lord.

Our lot establishes our line and reveals our inheritance. It determines the cup or the abundance from which we drink; this is the cup of the Lord. It determines the allotment for our portion of the inheritance.

As we walk on this earth, God gives us an assignment, and this assignment is our lot or our destiny. This is what we do; it is our lot in life. God has an assignment for you. He slips us an offer that says this is what will happen if you should choose to accept it. However, most people don't accept it; they think they want something else. Choose to live your life—your assignment, your lot—and refuse to play the lottery with your future.

THE WORD & THE SPIRIT

You find the mind of God in the Bible through His Spirit. The Bible gives you general instructions, but the Holy Spirit gives you the specifics. You can find out how to have a good marriage—general information that will speak to any couple. It will tell you what to do and how to go about it. However, the Bible will not tell you who to marry; it will not reveal the name of your life-partner. You choose your spouse by the unction, utterance, and leading of the Holy Spirit. For you to succeed in fulfilling God's destiny for your life, there are two things you must have:

1) You must be a student of the **Word** to have general instruction.

2) You must be a friend of the **Holy Spirit** to understand specific instruction.

Some might say, *"I don't think that will work for me."* If that statement is true, then God is a liar because He said it would work for His people. From John 10:3-5, Jesus promises, *"My sheep hear My voice and another they do not follow."* That is what He taught.

Every Christian has the ability to hear the voice of the Lord. You may fall short of hearing His voice, but that's not because

16

He's not talking. People don't hear His voice because they are not trained to hear it or don't practice what they have learned. You may not hear the voice of the Lord simply because you don't know how, or you are too young in the faith and too inexperienced about the things of God to understand how He speaks. You may not care anything about it and refuse to be still and quiet before Him. You must spend time with Him to become attuned to His voice, but I can assure you that failing to hear is not because God is failing to speak.

COOPERATING WITH YOUR DESTINY

3

SUCCESS IN GOD

The Bible says that the lines He gives us fall in pleasant places. That word "pleasant" means *delightful, sweet,* and *beautiful.* If you follow God's destiny—His lot for you or His plan for your life—it will take you to heaven. His plan not only promises that it will be pleasant in heaven, but it also promises some pretty good days here. Even with all its challenges, this Christian life is by far the best life you can live.

SUCCESS IN GOD'S EYES

If you follow God, He will lead you on a path of success and prosperity. However, these things do not always take the shape of your personal definition. A person who has accumulated vast amounts of money, influence, power, or prestige may be miserable, unhappy, and possibly dying from a dreadful disease brought on by the stress from achieving their many accomplishments. That kind of life does not fall into the box labeled "success and prosperity" in God's economy.

God is going to lead you to be productive and fulfilled. Money is merely a byproduct.

19

God has a way of measuring success and prosperity quite differently than you do. He said He would provide for you physically, but so often, our pursuits and our destiny seem to be wrapped up and hidden in money. I hear it said by scores of people, *"God's going to lead me to be rich!"* No, the correct statement is: God is going to lead you to be productive and fulfilled. Money is only a byproduct. The Bible tells us not to labor to be rich. If your pursuit is riches, you are not following the plan of God.

But will God make you rich? I believe so. Without reservation, the Scripture teaches that God wants all of us to have money; I do not have any problem with that part. However, if your goal and idea of success—at least coming from God—is only to have an abundance of money, you cannot possibly hear the voice of the Lord. You will be misled to the point of not knowing which end is up; the devil will run you around like crazy.

Without question, family, friends, relationships, church, productivity, wholeness, and peace are much more important than sacks full of money. God is not against money, but money is low on the goal meter. There is a godly goal that is a great deal higher.

It Won't Always Be Easy

Even though God wants your lines to be pleasant, delightful, sweet, bountiful, and beautiful, it does not mean the process will always be easy. The plan of God is where you will have a good and peaceful life in God—the God-life. But, if you take your life into your own hands and gamble with it, you are not going to like where you end up.

This verse talks about the destiny of Paul and Barnabas:

> As they ministered to the Lord, and fasted, the
> Holy Ghost said, Separate me Barnabas and
> Saul for the work whereunto I have called them
> (Acts 13:2).

In other words, God revealed to them that their lot was not where they thought it was. They thought it was all settled in place "A," when actually it was in place "B." God began to expand them.

There will be times when you think the lot you live on now is the only thing there is. God told the church, *"Separate Barnabas and Saul for the work I have called them."* Before that word, the lot of Barnabas and Saul was relatively small, but once that word came, their lot became bigger and bigger still.

With a large lot comes new and greater responsibility. A fresh anointing and favor came with their new mission to help them accomplish their goal. It wasn't just more money; it was more responsibility. Typically, more money comes with it, but their goal was not money alone.

The goal of their mission was delivering souls, building churches, and doing other mission work. Their goal was not money in and of itself; money is only a tool. I would never sell my soul for money. There is not enough money in this world to make you happy.

Their new assignment from God became their lot and destiny. You cannot take someone else's destiny; it is uniquely theirs.

God said to separate Paul (Saul) and Barnabas. They were in a group of prophets and teachers, and it did not include separating any of the others. When Paul and Barnabas were sent out, the others' lot did not change.

Colossians 4:17 says, "Take heed to the ministry which thou hast received in the Lord, that thou fulfil it." God gives us a lot, line, and destiny—a future, a heritage, and a cup. He also gives us all the things contained within those six words with the implication that we are to work inside that framework. God is saying, *"That is what I put you here to do; that is why you are here."*

The Bible says to take heed to the ministry or take heed to the destiny that you fulfill it. God gives it, but you have the responsibility to fulfill it. It is not automatic; you must do it. You must cooperate with His plan—walk in it and fulfill it. God's call is not going to happen just because God wills it; you must purpose or will to do it and work with it, as well. It is a joint effort. God gives us the plan, and we fulfill it.

TRUST GOD'S SUPPLY

For the most part, people do not like for preachers to talk about money, even though God talks about money. How on earth can you trust God with your destiny when you don't want to obey Him with the tithe? One might say, *"Lord, I'm trusting you with my whole future."* Okay, fine, then trust Him with that little part of your paycheck. Tithing will show where trust really lies. Where a man's treasure is, there is his heart. It is ludicrous to talk about trusting God with our whole eternity when we don't want to trust Him with ten percent of our paycheck!

Our subject is not tithing, but it is an essential topic in the context of our current discussion. People often don't tithe because of fear; they think they will lose whatever amount they tithe. However, you never lose what you put in God's hands; you keep it, and it stays in your life. What you spend down at the mall is what you lose. Tithing and giving demonstrate your trust in God for your future.

> For the body is not one member, but many. If the foot shall say, Because I am not the hand, I am not of the body; is it therefore not of the body? And if the ear shall say, Because I am not the eye, I am not of the body; is it therefore not of the body? If the whole body were an eye, where were the hearing? If the whole were hearing, where were the smelling? But now hath God set the members every one of them in the body, as it hath pleased him. And if they were all one member, where were the body? But now are they many members, yet but one body. And the eye cannot say unto the hand, I have no need of thee: nor again the head to the feet, I have no need of you. Nay, much more those members of the body, which seem to be more feeble, are necessary: And those members of the body, which we think to be less honourable, upon these we bestow more abundant honour; and our uncomely parts have more abundant comeliness. For our comely parts have no need: but God hath tempered the body together, having given more abundant honour to that part which lacked. That there should be no schism in the body; but that the

members should have the same care one for
another (1 Corinthians 12:14-25).

How can the hand say to the foot, *"I don't need you"*? How can
one body part tell another part, *"No one needs you"*? Each part
has a place and a job to do. The hand's assignment is not the
job of the foot, and vice versa. In the church, we often want to
choose the position of the foot, hand, or head. Jesus is the head
of the church, but sometimes we want that position, too.
Sometimes we want to make all the decisions; we don't want to
be an active part of the body. We may desire to make all the
choices, but that is God's job, not ours.

We want to be someone else. We want another person's
assignment—a different lot, and we want to work against God's
plan for our life yet enjoy His blessing in the middle of it. It just
does not work that way.

If you truly don't know how to find God's destiny for your life,
start asking Him about His plan for you. Just talk to Him
because He has a plan for everyone—you and me. His plan was
instituted before the foundation of the world, and it's a good
one. It will bring you fulfillment, peace, and unspeakable joy.

Jesus Himself said in John 4:34, "My meat is to do the will of
him that sent me, and to finish his work." There are many ways
that you can look at the word "meat." It can mean literally the
meat we eat, or it also means our earthly provision. **My meat or
my provision on earth is to do the will of God.**

Provision is going to be challenging when not pursuing the will
of God. Doing the will of God brings the provision of God
into your life. But if you dig a little deeper into that word

"meat," it can also mean satisfaction in life, contentment, joy, and all things related. It is the peace that passes all understanding.

Jesus was saying, *"Yes, earthly provision is a part of it, but your fulfillment and your contentment is also a part."* We don't just pursue the will of God; we finish the will of God. We find out what His plan is, and we do it; we work with it and never quit early. We finish it.

God did not call you to be famous, nor did He call you to be rich. He called you to do His will. However, if anything on that lot carries with it riches, fame, or any of those things, that's perfectly fine.

But you cannot become a squatter on another person's lot to get those things and maintain peace in your heart. There is a specific plan for your life, and you must cooperate with that plan by doing things His way and in His timing. Listen to His voice and then obey it. You must be a person of the Bible and led by the Spirit of God to find true success.

COOPERATING WITH YOUR DESTINY

4

UNDERSTANDING YOUR DESTINY

There are two main ways that people tend to think about destiny. The **first way** is that destiny is predestined; it is determined ahead of time. Therefore, it must happen because God required it. God mandated it, and there is nothing we can do to alter it; our destiny is as certain as the sun coming up in the morning. This is one thought.

I talked to a person not long ago who had lost someone close to them—and who was close to me as well. We found ourselves discussing our loss and the brevity of life. This person told me, "I believe that when it's your time, it's your time." That statement does not necessarily sound like it leads to predestination, but it really does. **It is a total violation of Scripture to believe there is a time for you to die that cannot be altered.**

Ponder this verse, "Honour thy father and thy mother: that thy days may be long upon the land which the Lord thy God giveth thee" (Exodus 20:12). The flip side of this truth is: dishonor your parents, and you will shorten your days on the earth. The Bible says you can do things that increase or decrease your days. Predestination believes that if it were decreed beforehand that tomorrow is your time to die, nothing could be done to change

27

it. However, the Scripture does not teach that at all. In fact, it teaches that there are many things you can do to lengthen or shorten your days.

God has a good plan for you, and He has something He wants to see you walk in, but your cooperation is required before you are going to walk in it. One theory about destiny says: it is basically all God and has nothing to do with me. Still, a **second way** of thinking says: it is all me and has nothing to do with God.

You cannot make your destiny happen. Remember the six words from Psalm 16 that we discussed in chapter one: *portion, inheritance, cup, lot, lines, and heritage?* You can't control any of them—none of them are up to you. These all come from somewhere else but not from you.

The Bible says you have a "lot" that God has given to you; it is your portion. Your lot determines your lines or boundaries, and your lines determine the size and shape of your lot. A surveyor can calculate the exact size and shape of your lot and tell you about restrictions associated with your property—like how close you can build to the edge of your lines, etc. Your life is very much like that because you have a lot in life—one that you did not choose—with which you have to work. You did not choose your race, IQ, gender, skin color, or era in which you were born; you were not involved in any of those decisions, but God was. Scripture says He had a plan for you before the foundation of the world, but that plan is not guaranteed to happen.

> Blessed be the God and Father of our Lord
> Jesus Christ, who hath blessed us with all

spiritual blessings in heavenly places in Christ: According as he hath chosen us in him before the foundation of the world, that we should be holy and without blame before him in love: Having predestinated us unto the adoption of children by Jesus Christ to himself, according to the good pleasure of his will, To the praise of the glory of his grace, wherein he hath made us accepted in the beloved. In whom we have redemption through his blood, the forgiveness of sins, according to the riches of his grace; Wherein he hath abounded toward us in all wisdom and prudence; Having made known unto us the mystery of his will, according to his good pleasure which he hath purposed in himself: (Ephesians 1:3-9).

Inside these lot lines of your destiny, there is plenty of wiggle room. You will need to make some serious choices regarding your limits, as these function as the limits or boundaries for your life. The Ten Commandments are an excellent example; they are limits that God imposed on our lives—do not kill, steal, lie, commit adultery, etc. If we stay inside those boundaries, we do well. If we stray outside of them, that is another conversation.

You have unique and specific lot lines for who you are because there are certain things God wants for you.

D-E-S-T-I-N-Y

I have been a conference leader in many **Destiny Conferences** all over the world. Our team formulated specific lessons that we taught to ensure people understood destiny. We developed an excellent acrostic for the word "destiny" that serves to define it.

D = Dream

In finding your destiny, God will give you a dream or a vision. We could call it that unique, wonderful, personal desire that God has given you for life. It is something that drives you in a way or intensity that does not drive others.

If you are going to find your destiny, you must have a dream and pursue it. Everyone has received a dream from God for some purpose, but everyone does not receive the same one. He has put a dream in every person fully compatible and consistent with their talents and developable skills. God is not going to give you a vision that is inconsistent with who you are. Knowing who you are will greatly influence the dream He gives you. Along with the dream, He gives you all the things it takes to realize it.

The dream God deposits in a person becomes the first inkling of their destiny.

E = Enthusiasm

God at work in you as evidenced by the dream He places in your heart. The dream energizes you and gives you enthusiasm for life that you would not have otherwise. You cannot have enthusiasm without a dream.

S = Single-Minded

Paul said, "This one thing I do (Philippians 3:13)." He did not say, *"These 101 things I do."* Life must have some focus and direction. The dream gives you focus that energizes your life.

T = Tomorrow and Today
I listed "tomorrow" first because tomorrow comes before today when you are pursuing your dream. The dream is taking you into your future, and the future will determine what you do with today. Therefore, **your tomorrow sets the course for what you do today.**

I = Impossible
Everything that God wants you to do is going to be impossible with men, so it requires you to call on Him. It requires you to trust Him. God is going to give you a dream that is impossible without Him but possible with Him.

N = Needs
God will not give you a dream that is self-centered and self-fulfilling to an end that would only make you wealthy and successful. He is going to give you a dream that helps other people. Through that dream, He will meet someone else's needs; you become the answer to their prayers.

Y = Yes
There is power in a "yes." In fact, nothing happens unless you say "yes." Mary had to say "yes," and the apostle Paul had to say "yes." When Peter was asked the question, *"Peter, will you follow me,"* he had to say "yes." If you do not say "yes," none of God's ability is activated—His resources do not move toward you. **The word "yes" has the power to attract the will of God to you.** That is important for you to remember.

GOD'S PLAN

God tells us:

"For I know the plans I have for you," declares
the Lord, "plans to prosper you and not to harm
you, plans to give you hope and a future"
(Jeremiah 29:11, NIV).

God has a unique plan for you. It is a good plan that will
prosper and bless you. Let's look again at a verse from Psalms:

Your eyes saw my unformed substance, and in
Your book all the days [of my life] were written
before ever they took shape, when as yet there
was none of them (Psalm 139:16, AMPC).

The Psalmist talks about the time before you were born,
formed, and placed on the earth. God had a plan that He
carved out for you before you were conceived. Never doubt that
you were well-conceived by the hand of the Lord, and you were
not an accident. You might have been an accident to someone,
but you were not an accident to the Lord. I know people with
large families who received an unplanned surprise. Well, it
might have been a surprise to them, but it was certainly not a
surprise to the Lord. He knew about it and even had a plan for
the child.

We could erroneously think of destiny as something we have no
control over, something God does all by Himself. Therefore, all
I must do is get in the boat, float down the river of life, and let
the divine current take me where it wants me to go. It may
come as a surprise to you, but you will end up locked down on
a sandbar or go rushing headlong over a waterfall if you take
that attitude. You will end up somewhere you do not want to
be—bound for the junk pile! However, the truth is that you
need to get the paddle out and do some serious rowing to orient
yourself toward God's favor.

The problem arises when we don't want God's chosen plan and try to do all the directing ourselves. But always remember: God gives us a lot—a portion, and the lot is a good one. For Christians, the real truth of destiny is that it is a partnership; it is not you alone, nor is it God alone. Destiny is you and God working together.

Doing what God chooses for us to do—what He put you on this planet to do—is the most important thing you could ever pursue.

Motivational speakers, sports coaches, and even parents often say, *"You can be anything you want to be!"* Unfortunately, and to their chagrin, that is simply not true. You can be what God gave you a lot in life to do because there is a lot just for you— a good plan of God's design. Being in the will of God is more important than making all the money on planet Earth. Doing what God chooses for us to do—what He put you on this planet to do—is the most important thing you could ever pursue. God has a plan, and when you cooperate with His plan, good things happen.

DON'T RELY ON LUCK

The word "lot" could be defined as a piece of ground or real estate, but it also carries with it the idea of chance or luck. Casting lots is an example. Luke 23:34b says, "And they parted his raiment and **cast lots**." It's hard to imagine, but there was gambling going on for Jesus' clothes. But, if you go to Las Vegas and play roulette, blackjack, or pull the arm on a slot machine, it is very much like casting lots. Interestingly enough, before the Day of Pentecost and before the Holy Spirit was poured out, you see people finding the will of God through casting lots of the *urim* and the *thummim* under the Old Covenant.

Before the Holy Spirit descended on people in Acts 2, Matthias was chosen as Judas' replacement by casting lots. In Acts 1, God's will was determined through casting lots. However, after Pentecost, everything changed. From Acts, chapter two onward, God's will was determined by the Spirit's leading. From that point on, casting lots was nothing but a distant memory.

I want you to see that God has a lot or a plan, but sometimes men follow their own path and gamble with their lives and futures. The word "lot" is the root or core word of lotto or lottery—playing a game of chance. When you do not follow the plan or submit to the lines or boundaries that God gives us, you are taking His place; you take God's role on yourself. At that point, you have decided, *"I will do it my way, and I will not have God intervene."*

Spirit-led people should say, *"Lord, what is your will for my life?"* You may have a plan, you may have a pursuit, but you must bring that under the oversight of the Lord. You can trust that God has a better plan for your life than you do. His plan will fulfill you and maneuver you to the right spot for your future. Did you know that some Bible translations indicate that "luck" is the root word for *Lucifer?* When you leave your life to chance, play your cards, or depend on luck to be your guide, just remember the root word for "luck." Who are you taking as your guide?

Life is not a game of chance. When we run our own lives, we roll the dice with our future and hope it works out. However,

Christians should not be living in a haphazard or chaotic way. God has a plan, and He wants to work it, but we must be willing to follow it.

LIVING THE GOOD "LOT"

There are several definitions for the word "lot." We know that a "lot" is a piece of ground on which you build a house or building. We also see that "lot" also plays a part in games of chance or luck—lotto or lottery. The definition upon which we want to focus is "that which is given to a person by divine providence—one's destiny or portion in life."

You have heard the phrase many times, "that's just their lot in life," referencing a person's portion or destiny. The good news is: God has a lot for us, and it is much better than what we could ever dream up.

Look at this New Testament reference to the children of Israel: "And when he had destroyed seven nations in the land of Canaan, he divided their land to them by lot" (Acts 13:19). In other words, the inheritance they received was determined by lots. They cast lots. Dan's portion was not the portion for Benjamin; it was different. If you try to live off someone else's vision, you are living on someone else's lot. God has one for you and one for me—they intermingle, yet they are different.

I think about Abraham, who is known as the father of our faith. His name was Abram, who had a name change by God to Abraham and became the father of our faith. At God's direction, Abram left his home without knowing exactly where He would end up. He only knew that he had to leave where he was, taking a select entourage with him.

35

COOPERATING WITH YOUR DESTINY

Sometimes your portion, lot, and destiny in life is the fulfillment of another person's destiny. Those people who followed Abraham would have never found their purpose in life if Abraham had disobeyed God.

When we follow God, we become the catalyst and the answer. We become the mechanism that allows others to find their destiny in God, which they would never realize otherwise.

Jesus said, *"Follow me, and I will **make you**."* When we follow Him, He makes us—that is the process. We must be followers of God, and we must listen to Him. As we understand our destiny, we see that it should not involve chance or luck, but God's guidance.

5

LIVING ON YOUR LOT

Our lot sets up our lines or boundaries. It establishes our inheritance and the cup from which we drink. It is our allotment or our portion of an inheritance. All those things that come from God are related to this concept of having a "lot." We all have a "lot" in life.

Your lot could be another way of saying your assignment or purpose—what you were put here to do. Remember, we are talking about destiny. How much of your future is yours to choose, and how much of it is God's plan? That is the question, isn't it? You cannot perform your destiny no matter how hard you try. You cannot make it happen by yourself. Furthermore, God will not do it without your cooperation.

GET COMFORTABLE WITH YOU

God has a good plan for you, and you need to get extremely satisfied and happy with it because you do not get a do-over. In fact, after the trump sounds and the earth and heavens have been renewed, and you find yourself one billion years into your eternity, you are still going to be you. You do not get a new you, so you better get happy with who you are because you have to be you for a long time to come. We all need to get comfortable in our own skin.

I am not saying that we don't need a little remodeling but make it simple. Get happy with who you are because you are stuck with that person forever.

Our training and preparation—education, relationships, social interactions, and career—**must** be in cooperation with the destiny God has for us. How do you know His plan? You discover it through what we refer to as the leading of the Spirit. God's Holy Spirit has a plan—a good plan, and you do not have to fear it. We must not take a chance with our future; we should very much want to be led by God.

THE HARD WAY

There's a good illustration in Acts:

> Now when the apostles which were at Jerusalem heard that Samaria had received the word of God, they sent unto them Peter and John: Who, when they were come down, prayed for them, that they might receive the Holy Ghost: (For as yet he was fallen upon none of them: only they were baptized in the name of the Lord Jesus.) Then laid they their hands on them, and they received the Holy Ghost. And when Simon saw that through laying on of the apostles' hands the Holy Ghost was given, he offered them money (Acts 8:14-18).

Simon had just been saved and delivered from the bonds of sorcery and witchcraft. He had been making money through the practice of witchcraft and controlling people's lives. As a result, he was seen as someone with prestige and possibly more spiritual insight than others. However, when he came to the Lord, nothing about his past was viable for him—it was no longer going to work. He didn't know that yet; he was still living as he did in the past. In this passage of Scripture, he saw that the Holy Spirit was given through the laying on of hands, so he offered them money to receive that kind of power.

> Saying, Give me also this power, that on whomsoever I lay hands, he may receive the Holy Ghost. But Peter said unto him, Thy money perish with thee, because thou hast thought that the gift of God may be purchased with money. Thou hast neither part nor lot in this matter: for thy heart is not right in the sight of God (Acts 8:19-21).

This passage describes the hard way we find ourselves going at times. We want to buy or borrow someone else's anointing, but you can't do that because an anointing is given by God.

Notice that Simon tried to buy his lot with money. He tried to replace his lot with a power that men could see. Simon wanted fame, prestige, and fortune—things related to earthly rewards—more than he wanted God's will. Peter's response was to tell him that his heart wasn't right in God's sight and that he would have no part or lot in the matter. Today, we would say, *"God did not give you this, pal. You tried to get it some other way."*

Your lot in life is given to you by God, not by someone else. Simon tried to do what the apostles were doing. The anointing the apostles walked in did not come quick or cheap. It was not a flimsy anointing; it was a holy, special, and unique thing.

> As they ministered to the Lord, and fasted, the
> Holy Ghost said, Separate me Barnabas and
> Saul for the work whereunto I have called them
> (Acts 13:2).

Once separated, there was a uniqueness that began to settle in
on Barnabas and Saul. One day they didn't have it, but the next
day they did. There were certain prophets and teachers in the
church who met together and prayed. They were separated
from the group and called apostles. None of the others were
called apostles.

"Well, I want to be an apostle, too!" Sorry, that's probably not your
lot. You can't buy this; it is given. What is my portion? What
are my lines? What are my boundaries? It is given by God and
God only. Your destiny is in God's hands, but you must
cooperate with it.

In the book of Acts, Peter told Simon:

> Thou hast neither part nor lot in this matter:
> for thy heart is not right in the sight of God.
> Repent therefore of this thy wickedness, and
> pray God, if perhaps the thought of thine heart
> may be forgiven thee (Acts 8:21-22).

He said you must repent from that way of thinking. When we
assume we can do something because we saw others do it or
because we have money, prestige, or connections, the command
is: "Repent." God has not given it to you. Repent. For
Christians, being in the will of God is doing what God has
called **us** to do.

KING SAUL'S MISTAKE

King Saul had a destiny, but he completely blew it. He rolled the dice with his life and his future by going to see the witch of Endor. Because of that mistake, his life ended up on the trash heap—in a giant mess. He lost his life because he sought the will of God through a false and phony source.

Saul did not seek God's will but the way of position. He sought prestige, power, and honor, which God would have gladly given. God was the One who called him to be king, but he pushed God out to do it his way through the lottery.

There is no quick way, including your own way, that wins in God's Kingdom. Today we hear about lottery winners—those who win the big money—who often find themselves on the junk pile of life a few years later. They end up much worse off than if they had never won the money, sometimes completely broke and destitute.

THE PLEASANT WAY

On the opposite side of this hard way, God tells us that the lines He gives fall in pleasant places.

> "The lines are fallen unto me in pleasant places;
> yea, I have a goodly heritage" (Psalm 16:6).

The word "pleasant" found in this verse means *delightful, sweet,* or *beautiful.* God has a good life—a peaceful life—designed for you. Pleasant places.

This verse tells us that God gives us boundaries for our lives, and if you cooperate with Him, those lines or boundaries will give you a good life. They will fall in pleasant places. That does not mean, however, that there are no difficulties, tests, trials, or challenges in life, but rather, God's plan for you will take you through the hard times to a pleasant place.

God did not come with a plan to destroy you. Instead, He came with a plan to fulfill you. He has a plan for your life that is consistent with what you have been given—your talents, giftings, connections—and His relationship to you. There are people who need you to be in God's will, which will, in turn, enable them to be in the will of God.

COMMISSIONED FOR BUSINESS

Several years ago, God spoke to me and my wife, Nora, and told us to start the church I currently pastor. One of the things the Lord said was that He wanted to build a people who were not then but now are. He wanted to make something exist out of something that did not exist.

Some business people may not know why they are in business. The number one reason God put you in business is to support His church. Because of that, God called you and wants to make you millionaires and bless you beyond measure. Your number one purpose is to finance His church; the church needs resources to do His work. God needs you to be part of a ministry. If you get that one thing straight, all the struggles will be over. God has drawn your lines in pleasant places. Your job is to line up your priorities in the proper order.

God has called businesspeople to bless His church. Some may think that's presumptuous. No, it's truthful. *"Well, He wants me to support my family."* Of course, He does, but that is not key. The key is found in the book of Matthew, and we'll look at three translations of the same verse:

> "But seek ye first the kingdom of God, and
> his righteousness; and all these things shall
> be added unto you" (Matthew 6:33, KJV).

> "But more than anything else, put God's work
> first and do what he wants. Then the other
> things will be yours as well" (Matthew 6:33, CEV).

> But first and most importantly seek (aim at,
> strive after) His kingdom and His
> righteousness [His way of doing and being
> right—the attitude and character of God], and
> all these things will be given to you also
> (Matthew 6:33, AMP).

If you seek God's Kingdom first, He will provide you with everything you need. This is the key.

OVERCOMING TEMPTATIONS

As people age and change, the things that are most important to us change as well. Up until the twenty-fifth or thirtieth year on the earth, it is all about sex. From thirty to about fifty, it is all about money. For the plus fifty crowd, it is all about health. Life always has temptations, but they change over the years.

> My son, if sinners entice thee, consent thou not. If they say, Come with us, let us lay wait for blood, let us lurk privily for the innocent without cause: Let us swallow them up alive as the grave; and whole, as those that go down into the pit: We shall find all precious substance, we shall fill our houses with spoil: Cast in thy lot among us; let us all have one purse: My son, walk not thou in the way with them; refrain thy foot from their path: (Proverbs 1:10-15).

This passage is talking about an enticement to do something wrong. If sinners entice you, we are not to listen to them. Now, the ultimate sin or sinner would be the devil, but he uses people to do his work. If the devil entices you, don't follow him.

Look again at the end of this passage: "We shall find all precious substance, we shall fill our houses with spoil" (Proverbs 1:13). In other words, there is a big payday coming on this one where you can get rich.

Enticing sinners beckon us: "Cast in thy lot among us" (Proverbs 1:14a). In other words, they are saying, *"Give your destiny to the pursuit of stuff. Give your destiny to the ways of the world. Cast your lot in with us."* The devil says, *"Do it my way, and I will make you rich. I will fill your house with wealth. I will fill you with all this nice stuff. You do it my way, and I will make you a star. I will make you somebody special. I will make you big. I will make you famous."* But this is what he really means, *"I will steal your soul now, and I will take you to hell in the end."* The devil leaves that part out. He says, "Cast in thy lot among us;

let us all have one purse." In other words: do it with me and do it my way.

In the next verse, we read, "My son, walk not thou in the way with them; refrain thy foot from their path" (Proverbs 1:15). Sin will try its best to take your destiny or your lot from you. Do not walk in it, do not follow it. God has a plan. It will take you to pleasant places. He has a good plan for you, and He wants to give it to you.

Colossians 4:17 says, "And say to Archippus, Take heed to the ministry which thou hast received in the Lord, that thou fulfil it." This verse says to take heed to the ministry that you have been given of the Lord, that you fulfill it. The Living Bible says it this way: "And say to Archippus, "Be sure that you do all the Lord has told you to" (Colossians 4:17, TLB).

Your ministry is your calling—your assignment. It is what you were put here to do. Take heed that you do it. Do not do something else—do what God called you to do. Live on your own lot.

COOPERATING WITH YOUR DESTINY

6

THE PLACE OF YOUR DESTINY

Let's look into the life of Abram and Sarai, whose names are later changed to Abraham and Sarah. Both of their names were changed and established by God for covenant reasons. So, from this point on, I will mainly use their God-given names of Abraham and Sarah. Only in their use in direct reference in Bible verses will they stay as the original Abram and Sarai. Hopefully, this will curtail any confusion. Let's look in Genesis 12:

> Now the Lord had said unto Abram, Get thee out of thy country, and from thy kindred, and from thy father's house, unto a land that I will shew thee: And I will make of thee a great nation, and I will bless thee, and make thy name great; and thou shalt be a blessing: And I will bless them that bless thee, and curse him that curseth thee: and in thee shall all families of the earth be blessed. So Abram departed, as the Lord had spoken unto him; and Lot went with him: and Abram was seventy and five years old when he departed out of Haran. And Abram took Sarai his wife, and Lot his brother's son, and all their substance that they

had gathered, and the souls that they had gotten in Haran; and they went forth to go into the land of Canaan; and into the land of Canaan they came. And Abram passed through the land unto the place of Sichem, unto the plain of Moreh. And the Canaanite was then in the land. And the Lord appeared unto Abram, and said, Unto thy seed will I give this land: and there builded he an altar unto the Lord, who appeared unto him. And he removed from thence unto a mountain on the east of Bethel, and pitched his tent, having Bethel on the west, and Hai on the east: and there he builded an altar unto the Lord, and called upon the name of the Lord. And Abram journeyed, going on still toward the south (Genesis 12:1-9).

This Scripture passage refers to the city of "Hai," which would be the city of Ai. For context, the children of Israel went into the Promised Land and overwhelmed Jericho but then were defeated in Ai. Hai is the same place as Ai.

The destiny that God has for you will be something that He, and not you, initiates.

It is revealing when a person steps into and follows the plan and purpose of God for their life. Notice in these verses that God initiated this pact; it was God who told Abraham there were things He wanted him to do. Likewise, the destiny that God has for you will be something that He, and not you, initiates. You just cannot say, *"I want to do this or that."*

There is a well-worn statement that we hear: You can be anything you want to be. Unfortunately, it is not true, because there are so many things over which you have no control. You had no control over where or at what moment in time you were born; you could have been born in 300 AD, the 1700s, or any other time. You did not choose the parents to whom you were born, your IQ, or the aptitudes God placed inside you. You did not influence the color of your skin or where you were born. You had no control over any of that; it was outside your purview and above your paygrade.

But what you do with what you have been given is of particular importance. You can't just sit on your hands and do nothing; you must work with what you have been given. You cannot be someone else, which goes back to your lot in life. Your lot determines your boundaries or your heritage, which are extremely important.

When God called Abraham, He gave four instructions:

1) Get out of the country or land where you currently live.
2) Leave your relatives, your family, and your birthplace.
3) Leave your father's house.
4) Go to a land that God would show you.

Concerning number three: Understand that you can leave your relatives, but not necessarily leave the house. You can live in your father's house but still be apart from the rest of your kinfolk. But God was saying that Abraham had to do something concerning both of those issues.

Then, the fourth instruction was to go to a land that God would show. There is a place God wants to show you. If you'll notice, Hebrews 11 says that Abraham did not know where he was going when he went out. He didn't know where to go, but he knew he couldn't stay where he was.

There are times when God does not tell us everything; He simply reveals something about the present that will take us to our future. In other words, we may not know exactly where we're going, but we know we're not staying where we are now. This revealing is just one of the ways—but not the only way—you will discover a bit of God's will. I have done some things I knew I would never do again soon after I did them because it wasn't for me. Certain things in life are just not for you.

GUIDANCE FOR YOUR JOURNEY

When God calls you to a place, position, or something new, there is a good chance that it is the Lord moving you. You may begin to experience an inclination or a warm feeling about it. The book of Acts says:

> **It seemed good unto us,** being assembled with one accord, to send chosen men unto you with our beloved Barnabas and Paul… For **it seemed good to the Holy Ghost, and to us,** to lay upon you no greater burden than these necessary things (Acts 15:25, 28, emphasis added).

The essence of this verse is saying, *"It seemed good to me at the time. It seemed good in the Holy Ghost. It seems right."*

However, you can't follow an unsubstantiated "right" feeling. If something seems right to you, you will need some confirming words to follow it. You will definitely want to get more than one if the pursuit is life-altering. **Significant decisions require extensive guidance**; they go together. If you are making huge, life-altering decisions, you need to get some huge guidance as you take each step forward.

- Small decisions = small guidance
- Big decisions = big guidance
- Life-altering decisions = HUGE guidance

If you are only going to the grocery store to buy a loaf of bread, big guidance is unnecessary. It's a small decision; just do it. However, if you are making big decisions that would affect and alter your life and the lives of others, you need big or HUGE guidance for those decisions.

Biblical precedence substantiates this truth: God does not call you to do something for Him without first telling you what He is going to do. When giving me instructions for an assignment, He has never failed to reveal His part to me.

God told Abraham to do some things: give up family, home, familiarity, and all the things that were his pillar or mainstay. God said, *"I want you to get rid of your security. I want you to move out in faith and trust Me."*

After specifying His instructions, God told Abraham that He would make him a great nation. God gave him a promise: *"If you do this, I will do that for you."* God put Himself on the hook. He said, if Abraham followed Him, among other things, He would make him a great nation. You can find this in Genesis:

> Now the Lord had said unto Abram, Get thee
> out of thy country, and from thy kindred, and
> from thy father's house, unto a land that I will
> shew thee: And I will make of thee a great
> nation, and I will bless thee, and make thy
> name great; and thou shalt be a blessing: And I
> will bless them that bless thee, and curse him
> that curseth thee: and in thee shall all families
> of the earth be blessed. So Abram departed, as
> the Lord had spoken unto him; and Lot went
> with him: and Abram was seventy and five years
> old when he departed out of Haran (Genesis
> 12:1-4).

God said that He would bless Abraham and make his name great. He does not say that to everyone, but He said that to him. God said He would make Abraham a blessing and bless those who blessed him and curse those who cursed him. With that, Abraham found himself with security in God, which meant protection. For you, it means you can go on your way trusting God; you can go to your new life, believing. The last thing God told Abraham was that all the families of the earth would be blessed through him. In effect, God was saying, *"If you do what I tell you, Abraham, I will do these things for you."*

That kind of blessing is the part of your destiny over which you have no control. The part of your destiny you can control is simply doing what God said to do. It's not tricky—obey God by doing what you were told to do. You cannot make a specific promise come to you. God initiates it, not you. However, you do have control over obeying what He says.

A PROMISE PASSED TO GENERATIONS

The New Testament tells us that Abraham's blessings have come on us through Christ Jesus. I get it, and you get it. To a degree, you can claim that, but you don't get to be Abraham. This specific promise was unique to him, and he was the one who had to obey. God did not say those words to everyone; He made this promise to Abraham alone.

We know that Abraham became the father of the Jewish nation, the Hebrews. The New Testament came from that, too. The Bible also says Abraham became the father of our faith by his obedience to the promise. When Scripture says all the families of the earth will be blessed, that is a direct reference that our Messiah, Jesus Christ, would come out of Abraham's loins.

Abraham was not going to personally or physically touch every person on the planet. He might influence them through the words he spoke and the heritage he left us, but he could not physically touch every human being. This passage says that God's manifested power, coming by means of Abraham's lineage through the person of Jesus Christ, would bless every person who accepts and embraces the Savior.

FOLLOWING AFTER GOD'S PROMISE

God told Abraham He would make his name great, and that certainly happened. Thousands of years later, we are still talking about Abraham and preaching about his life. God brought all that to pass.

Notice what the Bible says about this man:

> So Abram departed, as the Lord had spoken
> unto him; and Lot went with him: and Abram
> was seventy and five years old when he departed
> out of Haran (Genesis 12:4).

Abraham obeyed the Lord by leaving his home when he was 75 years old. Bear in mind that at 75, he is still moving in the plan and purpose of God. He is not worn out, giving up on life, or believing it is all over, but he is still hearing the voice of God and moving by His direction. At three-quarters of a century old, Abraham is moving out into the plan and purpose of God.

You need to follow God regardless of how many years you have lived on this earth. Your age should not stop you from hearing, obeying, and moving out in God. It doesn't matter how old you are; if you are on this planet, you still have a reason to be here. God is not finished with you yet.

Moses is another example of following God. He received his primary call from God when he was still a youngster of eighty years old. God spent those eighty years preparing Moses to lead the children of Israel out of Egypt and into the Promised Land. Then, the Lord's voice came from a burning bush and showed him why he was on this planet.

During his time in the wilderness tending sheep, I wonder how many times Moses gave up in his mind and wanted to take an early out to heaven. He led the children of Israel when he was 80 to 120 years old. After his calling and destiny were clear, at 120 years old, he lamented his inability to go on into the Promised Land. When it was time to go to heaven, Moses told God he did not want to go. At eighty years old, he had given up, but at 120, he was recharged, rekindled, re-anointed, and ready to press on.

When you realize God's destiny for your life, you are no longer tired, worn out, and ready to give up. Instead, you are champing at the bit to start, wanting to do more. When God speaks into our lives, He brings enthusiasm to bear. If you are not enthusiastic about life, it is because you are not walking in your destiny. Destiny brings enthusiasm.

> ## If you are not enthusiastic about life, it is because you are not walking in your destiny.

In his seventy-fifth year, Abraham determined to obey and follow God. Remember, while you are obeying the Lord, a lot of things unfold in time. I believe God does not show us everything at once because I don't think we could grasp or embrace it. We don't think we're ready for what's coming— and we're not.

But remember this: Along God's chosen path, He is maturing you to be ready for that crucial step when it comes. If you were privy to that step too early, you would know without question that you were not ready. So, be patient; it is not the time to deal with it. There is a great deal of maturing between where you are now and when your destiny is revealed, and you will be ready. That is why we trust and why we must listen.

In Genesis, it says:

> Now the Lord had said unto Abram, Get thee
> out of thy country, and from thy kindred, and
> from thy father's house, unto a land that I will

shew thee… And Abram took Sarai his wife, and Lot his brother's son, and all their substance that they had gathered, and the souls that they had gotten in Haran; and they went forth to go into the land of Canaan; and into the land of Canaan they came (Genesis 12:1, 5).

This is important. God told Abraham to leave his native country, relatives, and father's home and go to a new land where He would guide him. Even though he obeyed God, not knowing where he was going, he attempted to follow God.

But one of Abraham's first acts was disobedience to God. The Lord told him to go but not take any of his kin. What does Abraham do? Even after God specifically told him to take no one, Abraham took Lot, his nephew. He did the exact opposite of what God said to do. Abraham walked in partial obedience; he did go, but he took Lot with him. Abraham was discovering—just like we discover—that he wanted someone to help him out.

Even Moses told God that he was a man who could not speak well or talk effectively; he needed some help. So, God in His merciful nature told him to take Aaron to speak on his behalf. However, you cannot find anywhere in Scripture where Aaron actually spoke for him; Moses spoke for God himself. Humans tend to want a crutch. We want something to lean on, and God is not always opposed to it.

Notice that God told Abraham to get out of town and go to a land he would be shown (Genesis 12:1). This verse emphasizes an important truth. In and of itself, this verse requires future revelation. In other words, you have some knowledge today, but you are going to need more to fulfill God's will along the way. God told him, *"I am going to take you to a land, but I will show you where it is later."*

COOPERATING WITH YOUR DESTINY

7

A Place Called There

> And the Lord appeared unto Abram, and said,
> Unto thy seed will I give this land: and **there**
> builded he an altar unto the Lord, who
> appeared unto him (Genesis 12:7, emphasis
> added).

God told Abraham that He would show him where the land
was. When they finally got there, God said, *"There it is. I told
you I would show you the land. This is it."* At that time, Abraham
walked into the place where God took him.

There are three actions you must do to be in God's will and
perform His destiny:

- Do the right thing.
- Do it in the right way.
- Do it in the right place.

To be in God's will, you have the act, the method, and the
location—you cannot divorce yourself from any of these. You
can do the right thing the right way in the wrong place and get
nothing. You can do the wrong thing in the wrong way in the

right place and get nothing. You can do the right thing the wrong way in the right place and get nothing.

You have no choice but to do the right thing, in the right way, and in the right place.

There is a place in our life called "there." This is the place of your destiny, but so many people never find it. They never find what God wants them to do. Even though they sense what God intends for them to do with their life, they never position themselves to perform it.

I heard a respected minister say that the Lord spoke to him very clearly that 80 to 85 percent of all preachers never get into the will of God. Preachers that go preach just to do something, rather than specifically do what God told them to do in the place where God told them to do it.

Brother Kenneth Hagin said he went into the field after about twelve years of pastoral ministry experience. At that point, God told him that he was just now entering his first phase of ministry—after 12 years of dutiful service. God was saying, *"You have been doing the right thing, even doing it the right way, but you are just doing it in the wrong place."*

Destiny requires all of that. All of those things must come into place—right thing, right way, and right place. There is a place called "there."

YOUR ALTAR

Abraham built an altar in the land where God told him. Often in the church today, we have traded the altar for the stage.

Many have become performance-oriented rather than God-oriented. An altar is a place of exchange—a place where God and man do business. It is a place of bargaining, covenant, and worship. It is all those things, but it does not have to be elaborate.

In the case of Abraham, the altar was nothing more than a pile of rocks that he piled up and declared, *"This is the place where God said something to me. I heard it, and I believe it, and I honor the word that the Lord spoke."* It was a place of business—a place of exchange.

Every person needs an altar.

Every person needs a place where the world cannot intrude—a place where we come into the presence of God to do business with Him. It is a place where you state your case, and God makes His case. It is a place where we receive from Him. It is a place where we make statements and requests. It is a place of interaction, a place of business, a place of exchange, and a place of acknowledgment of that exchange. Therefore, because of the sacredness of those things, we make it a place of worship. It does not have to be elaborate or ornate. It can be the corner of a room. It is just a place where I acknowledge that God and I meet there, and we talk.

GOING ON STILL

In this story, I want you to see something of significance. Abraham is moving in the will of God; he obeyed God when he left his home. God told him to go to a land that He would show him. Abraham is physically in the land where God directed him.

Notice this pivotal verse: "And Abram journeyed, going on still toward the south" (Genesis 12:9). Abraham went out, not knowing where; he was going to a place God promised to show him. But when he got to the place that God showed him, he traveled still further. Mistake. When you get to the place where God is taking you, stop; don't keep moving.

But Abraham, who was still learning, went on further. I don't think he was trying to disobey God on purpose—that was not his motivation. Abraham was learning how to follow the will of the Lord. In the process of discerning God's will, he came to the place of blessing; the place where your enemies cannot get to you. He came to the place where all those things that God promised were going to happen. When you get to that place, you stop; go no further.

And when he got there, he thought, *"Well, I have been moving for a while. I'm used to this nomad lifestyle. I like moving when I want to move, and going where I want to go, being free in the Lord. So, I am going to keep on going."* When he kept going, however, some less than stellar things began to happen. Let's look at this verse in context:

> And Abram journeyed, going on still toward the south. And there was a famine in the land: and Abram went down into Egypt to sojourn there; for the famine was grievous in the land (Genesis 12:9-10).

The famine may have happened anyway, but there was nothing said about it until after Abram continued on. Whatever the case, he kept going and found himself in a famine.

In the same way, God plants you in a church and puts you in a place where you are fed the Word of God, where you are growing and flourishing, where your life begins to unfold into what God wants it to be, and then you go on still—as the Scripture says. You begin to search for something. For what? A new will of God? You are playing the lottery with your life instead of taking the lot that God has given to you. That is when you begin to do **your** will instead of obeying **His** will.

There was a famine in the land, and because of it, Abram went down into Egypt. In Scripture, Egypt is always a type of the world and sin; you never want to go to Egypt. You go up to Jerusalem, and you go down to Egypt. That is what you find in the Scripture. You go up to the promises of God and go down when you leave them. So, Abraham went down, and things happened. A conflict arose between Lot's and Abraham's herdsmen because of how much each group had been blessed. They were so incredibly blessed that the land could no longer satisfy the vast numbers of livestock. Because of this, the herdsmen bickered back and forth.

As a result, Abraham went to Lot and said, *"I don't want there to be any strife among us; we are brethren. Just look out there and take whatever land you want."* Abraham gave Lot "first dibs" or the first choice of land. With that option, Lot took the best fields, and certain things began to happen.

His Wife Became His Sister

Abraham and Sarah were of advanced years when they went down to Egypt. Abraham had to devise a plan. If you will remember, Sarah was exceptionally stunning and looked much younger than her sixty-five years. The Bible says that because

Sarah was so beautiful, there was a great possibility that Pharaoh and those in his house might want to marry her. So, Abram said, *"Now, when we go down there, Sarah, I want you to tell everyone you see that you are my sister. Because you are so pretty, they may want to take you as their wife, and then it will get us all in trouble. They may kill me to get you."*

When they arrived, just as Abram said, Pharaoh took Sarah, and consequences began to happen in his house.

> And it came to pass, that, when Abram was come into Egypt, the Egyptians beheld the woman that she was very fair. The princes also of Pharaoh saw her, and commended her before Pharaoh: and the woman was taken into Pharaoh's house. And he entreated Abram well for her sake: and he had sheep, and oxen, and he asses, and menservants, and maidservants, and she asses, and camels. And the Lord plagued Pharaoh and his house with great plagues because of Sarai Abram's wife (Genesis 12:14-17).

Now, remember what the Bible said earlier in this chapter:

> And I will make of thee [Abram] a great nation, and I will bless thee, and make thy name great; and thou shalt be a blessing: And I will bless them that bless thee, and curse him that curseth thee: and in thee shall all families of the earth be blessed (Genesis 12:2-3).

Another translation records God saying:

> I will bless you and make your descendants into
> a great nation. You will become famous and be
> a blessing to others. I will bless anyone who
> blesses you, but I will put a curse on anyone
> who puts a curse on you. Everyone on earth
> will be blessed because of you (Genesis 12:2-3,
> CEV).

When Abraham walked out of the destiny that God prepared
for him and went away from the land that God provided, it
began to cause things around him to go haywire. He began to
go his own way and do his own thing. Abraham decided to roll
the dice and play the lottery with his life—take his life into his
own hands rather than do what God told him to do.

Through Abraham's actions, Pharaoh ended up cursed. Why
did it happen to Pharaoh? When you step out of the will of
God, it does not only affect you; what was intended to be a
blessing to those around you now becomes a curse to them. It
affects everyone around you. Pharaoh is now walking under the
curse of Almighty God because of Abraham's disobedience.

You say, *"Well, that's not fair to Pharaoh."* You can talk to God
about that because I didn't write it. I don't know the inner
workings of all that, but I guarantee you it's in there.

RICHES CAN GET YOU OUT OF GOD'S WILL

Then we get into Genesis 13 and again find this situation
involving Abraham and Lot. The Bible says, "And Abram was

very rich in cattle, in silver, and in gold" (Genesis 13:2). The wealth they were experiencing was the reason they separated.

> But the land couldn't support both of them; they had too many possessions. They couldn't both live there—quarrels broke out between Abram's shepherds and Lot's shepherds (Genesis 13:6, MSG).

The point is: Poverty does not always mark a step out of the will of God. In fact, one of the things that satan uses to pull you out of the will of God is the promise of great riches. Here we find Abraham absolutely out of the will of God, but he was extraordinarily rich in cattle, silver, and gold.

I have watched people over the years and seen this more times than I can count. People begin to move in the plan of God, rolling up their sleeves and getting active in the Kingdom. But the next thing you know, a promotion comes their way that requires a career alteration. I have seen more people taken out of the will of God by the promise and allurement of money than any other single thing. Even though they are moving in God, living in the best spiritual place they have ever been, yet they will sell it all out to **go on still**. By their actions, they are saying, *"I know that this is the place, but I'm going to keep on going."*

Why? Why? Why? All for the promise of stuff! Here is the problem of making decisions based on money or things: You will not be judged or rewarded in heaven by how much you accumulate on earth. In fact, as Nora and I became aware of the will of God early in our marriage, it was a major setback financially. However, if a man will lose his life, he will find it. The Amplified Bible says it like this:

> For whoever wishes to save his life [in this world] will [eventually] lose it [through death], but **whoever loses his life [in this world] for My sake will find it [that is, life with Me for all eternity]** (Matthew 16:25, AMP, emphasis added).

Finances are often the worst guide that you can have. It can deceive you completely. Satan is the god of this world, and that is why God said you cannot serve God and money. Money is a corrupt god. God cares about your money, but it is not your god. Money should never lead you.

There are times you must position yourself to do what God called you to do. You cannot serve God and money. You must get that straight. If you allow it, money will get in the way of your obedience to God every single time. It is a tool that satan uses to maneuver and manipulate you and take you straight out of God's will.

How to Follow God

We can learn how to follow God as we read the Bible. When we follow the destiny God has for us, we must remember three things. The **first** thing to remember is that God has a place of blessing. Let's look at Genesis 13 in more depth, where we find this unfolding saga of Abraham and Lot:

And Abram went up out of Egypt, he, and his wife, and all that he had, and Lot with him, into the south. And Abram was very rich in cattle, in silver, and in gold. And he went on his journeys from the south even to Bethel, unto the place where his tent had been at the beginning, between Bethel and Hai; Unto the place of the altar, which he had make there at the first: and there Abram called on the name of the Lord. And Lot also, which went with Abram, had flocks, and herds, and tents. And the land was not able to bear them, that they might dwell together: for their substance was great, so that they could not dwell together. And there was a strife between the herdmen of Abram's cattle and the herdmen of Lot's cattle: and the Canaanite and the Perizzite dwelled then in the land. And Abram said unto Lot, Let there be no strife, I pray thee, between me and thee, and between my herdmen and thy herdmen; for we be brethren. Is not the whole land before thee? separate thyself, I pray thee, from me: if thou wilt take the left hand, then I will go to the right; or if thou depart to the right hand, then I will go to the left. And Lot lifted up his eyes, and beheld all the plain of Jordan, that it was well watered every where, before the Lord destroyed Sodom and Gomorrah, even as the garden of the Lord, like the land of Egypt, as thou comest unto Zoar. Then Lot chose him all the plain of Jordan; and Lot journeyed east: and they separated themselves the one from the other. Abram dwelled in the land of Canaan, and Lot dwelled in the cities of the plain, and pitched his tent toward Sodom. But the men of Sodom were wicked and sinners before the Lord exceedingly. And the Lord said unto Abram, after that Lot was separated from him, Lift up now thine eyes, and look from the place where thou art northward, and southward, and eastward, and westward: For all the land which thou seest, to thee will I give it, and to thy seed for ever. And I will make thy seed as the dust of the earth: so that if a man can number the dust of the earth, then shall thy seed also be numbered. Arise, walk through the land in the length of it and in the breadth of it; for I will give it unto thee (Genesis 13:1-17).

God wanted to take Abraham to the place of blessing, but Abraham and Lot found themselves separated because of their prosperity. It was here that Abraham took one more step to be in compliance with God's initial command, *"Get thee out of this place unto a place I will show you and get rid of your kinfolk and follow me."* So here, when they separated, it was one more step toward his destiny.

Notice what happened when Abraham separated from his nephew: Lot went toward Sodom and Gomorrah, and you know how that worked out. The Scripture says Lot pitched his tent toward (or facing) Sodom because that is where he wanted to look. He could have turned the back of his tent toward Sodom, but instead, he made sure the flaps opened with Sodom in full view. The Bible says the men of Sodom were wicked.

Let's look at a different translation to see what God told Abraham after separating from Lot:

> After Abram and Lot had gone their separate ways, the Lord said to Abram: Look around to the north, south, east, and west. I will give you and your family all the land you can see. It will be theirs forever! I will give you more descendants than there are specks of dust on the earth, and someday it will be easier to count the specks of dust than to count your descendants. Now walk back and forth across the land, because I am giving it to you (Genesis 13:14-17, CEV).

What I want you to notice is the blessing. The destiny of God began to be fulfilled for Abraham when he obeyed what God told him to do and separated himself from Lot. There is probably a number of reasons for that. One possible reason could be that they did not yet have an heir—Sarah was barren. Abraham might have given the whole covenant to Lot, his nephew. We don't know that, but it's possible.

You cannot tell God what He must do concerning your destiny. If Abraham had stayed with Lot, the indication here is that the promise God swore to Abraham—*"Look around, everything you see, I am going to give it to you"*—would have been negated. In fact, that word from God would have never come to him in the first place had he not separated from Lot.

In the next chapter, we learn that Abraham had to rescue Lot when the kings overcame him and took his possessions. Abraham came to his aid:

When Abram learned that Lot had been captured, he called together the men born into his household, 318 of them in all, and chased after the retiring army as far as Dan. He divided his men and attacked during the night from several directions, and pursued the fleeing army to Hobah, north of Damascus, and recovered everything—the loot that had been taken, his relative Lot, and all of Lot's possessions, including the women and other captives. As Abram returned from his strike against Chedorlaomer and the other kings at the valley of Shaveh (later called King's Valley), the king of Sodom came out to meet him, and Melchizedek, the king of Salem (Jerusalem), who was a priest of the God of Highest Heaven, brought him bread and wine. Then Melchizedek blessed Abram with this blessing: "The blessing of the supreme God, Creator of heaven and earth, be upon you, Abram; and blessed be God, who has delivered your enemies over to you." Then Abram gave Melchizedek a tenth of all the loot. The king of Sodom told him, "Just give me back my people who were captured; keep for yourself the booty stolen from my city." But Abram replied, "I have solemnly promised Jehovah, the supreme God, Creator of heaven and earth, that I will not take so much as a single thread from you, lest you say, 'Abram is rich because of what I gave him!' All I'll accept is what these young men of mine have eaten; but give a share of the loot to Aner, Eshcol, and Mamre, my allies" (Genesis 14:14-24, TLB).

71

Scripture tells us that after Abram brought Lot's possessions back, he gave a tithe—ten percent of everything—to Melchizedek. When the King of Sodom told Abram to keep everything but the people, Abram said, *"No thanks."* He didn't want it to be said that any person made him rich; God Almighty alone made him rich.

Abram's future and his fate were in God's hands; he was not going to roll the dice with his future. After Abram rescued Lot and tithed of all his substance, he had a vision as described in this verse:

> After these things the word of the Lord came unto Abram in a vision, saying, Fear not, Abram: I am thy shield, and thy exceeding great reward (Genesis 15:1).

After the vision, God made a covenant with Abram:

> In the same day the Lord made a covenant with Abram, saying, Unto thy seed have I given this land, from the river of Egypt unto the great river, the river Euphrates: (Genesis 15:18).

After Abram obeyed God and tithed from his substance, God's future promise became an upgrade to his covenant. God swore that what He promised Abram would also happen for you and to you.

Let me tell you something about your destiny: God has it, and He holds it. You must cooperate with Him to go to the place of blessing. Abraham obeyed because he had a word from the Lord that would take him to a place of blessing.

Secondly, when you follow God, remember to follow Him fully and precisely. When Abram initially left his home, he was not fully obedient; he took Lot with him. Abram learned obedience through the things He suffered. That trip to Egypt did not work out well. When he left Egypt, Scripture says he had to go back to the exact same place that God had told him not to leave. God did not give him a new place; Abraham had to go back to "there." He could have saved himself boatloads of trouble by simply staying put.

Do not go further than God tells you to go.

The **third** thing to remember in following God is to avoid presumption. After God showed him his place, Abram continued to move. He got antsy—anxious, impatient, or eager. He stepped out with no word from God.

It was a bit like Moses. On the way to the Promised Land, Moses was tasked with the responsibility of finding water for the people. God told him to smite a rock, and after Moses was obedient and smacked it, the water gushed out. The second time around, he presumptuously smote the rock before listening to what God said to do; God did not tell him to strike it a second time. Moses' disobedience cost him severely.

God gave Abram a word, and Abraham made it a sentence. Likewise, when God gives us a word, we tend to make sentences from it as well. We go on from where He told us to stop. We assume the blessing that got us to that point is a blessing that will take us forward. Not so fast; be patient. You move in God again and again, but when you get presumptuous and quit asking and move on anyway, you are getting ready to go to Egypt. Just because He gave you His will at the beginning does not mean you do not need to continue to ask.

Abram had to go back to the original place of his disobedience. When we follow God, we must also move in His will. Moses was presumptuous when he smote that rock the second time. The rock was a type of Christ, and Christ was smitten only once for our sin, not twice. Because of Moses' disobedience by smiting that rock twice, he did not get to enter the Promised Land in the way God intended it. He stepped out of his destiny by presumption—the same as Abraham stepped out of his. That is the same way we do it. Sometimes we inquire of the Lord, but we make assumptions and go on and do whatever we want.

In summary, we must realize there is a place of blessing where God is leading us. We must obey His instructions fully and precisely—not partially, and we cannot be presumptuous with our movements and our motions. We must recognize that He is working on a greater plan than we can even comprehend. We do not see all things, just like Abraham did not see all the ramifications of the blessing. He did not see us. He did not see what God saw. That is why you must follow Him.

We must trust God with our destiny and our future. Sometimes we just have to step out in faith, but we are not stepping out in faith to aimlessly drift without hope. We may not see it all, but God has a definite place for our destiny to take root and come to fruition—a place called there.

8

PEOPLE OF DESTINY AVOID STRIFE

How do you become a people of destiny? God has a plan, and we, as His partners, share in some give and take with Him. It is not all God's responsibility with no obligation on our part, and it certainly is not all our responsibility. Remember, if we take our lot, our inheritance, our portion, or our part into our own hands, it goes back to that concept of the lottery. In that case, I hope it works out for you. Go ahead and spin the wheel and roll the dice because that is what's in store for you if you try to manage or administer your destiny on your own without God's involvement. God has a wonderful portion that He wants to give us, but we must cooperate with Him.

There are many people in our destiny. God told Abram to leave his kinfolk behind. What did he do? He took Lot: right thing, right place, wrong way. However, as they journeyed, God began to prosper them, and they had herds, flocks, and tents.

Abraham and Lot became so prosperous by the hand of the Lord that they had to separate. There were far too many sheep, cattle, and other livestock trying to co-exist on the same pastures. When Lot was taken prisoner in a battle, Abraham went down to set him free. After he took possession of the spoils of war, he made this statement, *"Let no man say he has*

COOPERATING WITH YOUR DESTINY

made Abraham rich but God Almighty." He knew from where his
blessing had come. He was wealthy by the hand of the Lord.

> And there was a strife between the herdmen of
> Abram's cattle and the herdmen of Lot's cattle:
> and the Canaanite and the Perizzite dwelled
> then in the land. And Abram said unto Lot, Let
> there be no strife, I pray thee, between me and
> thee, and between my herdmen and thy
> herdmen; for we be brethren. Is not the whole
> land before thee? separate thyself, I pray thee,
> from me: if thou wilt take the left hand, then I
> will go to the right: or if thou depart to the right
> hand, then I will go to the left (Genesis 13:7-9).

Abraham was so confident of God's supply that he told Lot in
today's vernacular, *"Just take whichever looks best to you. I don't
care; God will prosper me wherever I go."* Lot took the best area,
but that led him to a place he did not need to go. He ended up
pitching his tent toward Sodom. We know that decision didn't
work out well for him.

The point I want to make clear is that strife arose between Lot's
herders and Abraham's herders because of the things I just
described. There was not enough room for everything to take
place; the land had grown too small for the blessing that was on
their lives.

Abraham said, "Let there be no strife, I pray thee, between me
and thee" (Genesis 13:8). He was aware of the strife running
through the camp over this issue, and he knew it was critical for
him not to allow it to take the blessing of God from them. We

76

can see Abraham walking in biblical maturity beyond his understanding. He didn't have the New Testament to turn to like we do, but somehow, he understood these godly principles.

Abraham refused to allow the herder's strife to come between them; he stepped in to end the strife before it had time to mature and manifest. With regard to the harsh words people speak to one another, the Bible says "their word will eat as doth a canker" (2 Timothy 2:17). Strife grows, but Abraham stopped it.

People can instigate rumors and accuse one another. They can allow their discontentment to cloud their good judgment. Abraham said we must keep strife away if we are going to have the blessing of God on our lives. He said: *"Let there be NO strife between me and you."* We are talking about being a people of destiny. Strife could have stopped Abraham and Lot's destiny. Strife is a killer.

If we keep strife at bay, we can maintain our peace. We do not need to let strife of any kind establish a foothold in our lives. We need to squelch and calm the strife in the camp. People need to see us live in harmony. Abraham viewed his nephew as an equal and referred to him as a brother. He said, *"Let's act right; let us act like brothers."*

To eliminate the strife, Abraham went to Lot. The Scripture tells us that if someone has an ought or offense against you, go and be reconciled to your brother.

> Therefore if thou bring thy gift to the altar, and
> there rememberest that thy brother hath ought

against thee; Leave there thy gift before the
altar, and go thy way; **first be reconciled to thy
brother, and then come and offer thy gift**
(Matthew 5:23-24, emphasis added).

It is time to reconcile instead of letting strife fester. We need
to keep in mind that we are talking about fulfilling your destiny
and the strategies that the enemy uses to take you out of it.

YOU MUST BE IN THE RIGHT PLACE

It is essential that you be in the right place. You cannot just
accomplish your destiny anywhere. You simply cannot jump
into your destiny if you are in the wrong place. If God has
connected you to someone or something—a situation or your
local church—stay there; this is your plug-in point to the body
of Christ. Once you find where you are supposed to be, the
devil will try to bring strife from other places into your life to
take you out of your destiny. You might say, *"Well, I can do this
in another church."* Really? I thought there was a place of destiny.

Some situations require a church change. At times like that,
you must ask: where am I getting spiritual food. God does not
want you in a church where you know more than the pastor. In
my life, there were times when I had to change because I
realized that it was not working. Rather than possibly getting
into strife, I had to obey God. I felt somewhat like Abraham,
coming out of the land he was used to without a clue where he
was going. Sometimes you do not know where the land is; you
just know where the land is not. You feel like, *"I can't do that
anymore. The cost is too high to stay there."*

There are ways to discern where you need to be going to
church. Are you fed with good groceries—fed with the correct

doctrines? If you are tithing to a church that tells you speaking in tongues is of the devil, you are as guilty as the one who said the words because you support that incorrect doctrine. The Bible says if you bless a person who is not walking with God, you are guilty of their same sin. In that situation, you must decide what you need to do.

I believe in walking in love and harmony, but sometimes I can do that much easier at a distance. Let there be peace. *Kumbaya,* ya'll. When you begin to get in that place where you start to receive from God, one of the things that the enemy will do is bring many opportunities your way to lead you into strife.

OPPORTUNITIES FOR STRIFE

Strife comes in a variety of ways, and one common path to it is **offense**. I hate to tell you this, but church people can still get offended. How does God correct us? He uses the Word of God to correct us when we are going the wrong way. When we hear a Scripture, we must understand that it was read from God's Holy Word. The pastor didn't write it; it's not original with them. You must pause when you are going through a correction from the Lord to allow time for it to be completed. You cannot get angry at the messenger or God if He is dealing with you.

Sometimes people get offended or are separated from their destiny because of unrealistic expectations. In this world, many people expect things from the church or others that are not their responsibility to fulfill. For instance, it is not the church's role to make you wealthy; instead, the opposite is true; it is your role to enrich the church. Christians are the ones ordained by God to bring substance into God's house.

The pastor is the one who is supposed to teach you how to be successful. Pastors must teach principles that cause your life to succeed, but then you must implement those principles. Through that process, God begins to raise you up and increase you. However, some expect the church to meet many of their needs. Those people say things like, *"Well, my needs are not being met. The church is not meeting my needs."* I hate to tell you this, but you are the church. The structure where you meet is not the church; you are the church. God never said, *"Come in here and expect your needs to be met,"* He said, *"Come in here and help someone else get their needs met."* That is your role, then look to Him for what you can't do.

When people allow their feelings to be hurt, they tend to reverse the roles and develop unrealistic and unfair expectations. *"I got my feelings hurt when I went to church there. Somebody did this and did that, and it really upset me."* The truth is, you had an expectation of what was supposed to happen, and it may not have been biblical. You must grow in God according to the Word of God; then all that other stuff gets in line. The church should be important in people's lives when they get into trouble or fall on hard times, but grandiose expectations on behalf of church members are out of order. I'll end this thought by saying that the Scripture does say if a man does not work, neither should he eat (2 Thessalonians 3:10). I'll let you ponder that.

So, Abraham recognized the power of strife and tried to end it, and he called Lot his "brother." He went to him as an equal, not as a condescending uncle to a young nephew, not the elder to the younger, but as brother to brother.

These principles are articulated in the book of James, which tells us something quite important:

Who is a wise man and endued with knowledge among you? Let him shew out of a good conversation his works with meekness of wisdom. But if ye had bitter envying and strife in your hearts, glory not, and lie not against the truth. This wisdom descendeth not from above, but is earthly, sensual, devilish. For where envying and strife is, there is confusion and every evil work (James 3:13-16).

Abraham was aware of that principle. He was saying, *"Envy and strife reign in this arena where we are living; every evil thing under the sun is going to enter in here."* That is precisely what is being said. If strife rules the day, you cannot stop the rest of evil from coming into the situation.

In the Modern English Version, James 3:16 says, "For where there is envying and strife, there is confusion and every evil work" (MEV). Strife becomes the seed and core. If we do not deal with it in the beginning, then we will watch it spring up all over the place. Remember, I am talking about destiny. I am talking about walking in the plan and the path God has for your life. Here is a classic example of Abraham knowing that if he doesn't deal with strife, neither he nor Lot will get to where they need to be in God. God has a plan, but the enemy has a different strategy to sabotage the will of God in our lives.

Look closely at this passage in James 3. Strife leads to false wisdom. In James 3:15, the Bible refers to this wisdom as earthly (it comes from around you), sensual (through your senses), and devilish. However, we need to draw our wisdom from God.

We see where strife creates confusion. When you are in strife, you cannot hear the voice of God. It will create confusion, both externally and internally. If you have internal chaos, you can't discern the voice of the Lord, which is how people get deceived.

People try to justify strife; they try to justify contention. *"Well, I'm entitled."* No, you are not. If anybody is entitled to walk in unforgiveness, it would be the Lord because He never sinned. But He does not walk in unforgiveness; He forgives us if we come to Him. He is our example. Abraham knew to avoid strife because it was a killer and had to be eliminated.

THE TEAM OF PAUL & BARNABAS

Let's look at this story found in Acts 13:

> Now there were in the church that was at Antioch certain prophets and teachers; as Barnabas, and Simeon that was called Niger, and Lucius of Cyrene, and Manaen, which had been brought up with Herod the tetrarch, and Saul. As they ministered to the Lord, and fasted, the Holy Ghost said, Separate me Barnabas and Saul for the work whereunto I have called them. And when they had fasted and prayed, and laid their hands on them, they sent them away (Acts 13:1-3).

We find Barnabas and Paul referred to as teachers or prophets; they fulfilled one or both roles. We know later that Paul was appointed as an apostle and was identified with that title from that time forward. The church recognized a higher, deeper, and stronger calling on Paul and Barnabas to step out of their previous roles because they alone, and none of the others, were asked to make a move.

Paul and Barnabas moved into their apostolic role immediately. They were elevated to the office of the apostle, recognized in the position, and sent by the church to fulfill that mission. Would you say they are stepping into a deeper portion of their destiny? They are on the path; it was God that summoned them. They were called to step into the role of the apostle, and the Holy Spirit separated them to do so.

To **separate** means "to set off by boundary," which goes right back to the concept of the lot—which also means to set off by a boundary. Paul's boundaries included the role of the apostle; that was his lot. It means to appoint, to declare, or to ordain.

Notice what Luke writes, "After these things the Lord appointed other seventy also, and sent them two and two before his face into every city and place, whither he himself would come" (Luke 10:1). The principle God used when sending people out was to send them two-by-two; it makes a lot of sense because there is safety in that number. Not only is it logical, but there are spiritual components: the power of agreement, the power of protection, and the availability of one to watch the other's back. Many good things happen when we go together in one accord.

In Acts 13, God set up a two-man team. Paul and Barnabas were set apart by the Holy Spirit to be a team and set apart by the hand of God to go out and do the work of the Kingdom together. It was not man's doing; it was God's doing. They were fasting and praying when the Holy Ghost said, *"Separate these two, I have a mission for them, and they are to go together."*

The Scripture says:

> And some days after Paul said unto Barnabas,
> Let us go again and visit our brethren in every
> city where we have preached the word of the
> Lord, and see how they do. And Barnabas
> determined to take with them John, whose
> surname was Mark. But Paul thought not good
> to take him with them, who departed from
> them from Pamphylia, and went not with them
> to the work (Acts 15:36-38).

Paul had a revelation that they needed to check on the work they had started, and Barnabas determined that they needed to take John Mark. However, the problem with John Mark was they had traveled with him before, and he had jumped ship, possibly due to immaturity or a lack of discipline, leaving them in a lurch. When you are on the mission field, you can't run the risk of a mental, physical, or maturity breakdown when everything needs to go a certain way.

I have traveled over much of the world and been to over 60 countries. I have been with both large teams of people and alone. Sometimes being without a team is better than being with one person. There are some environments where you are better off without taking extra people for various reasons: the need for food, shelter, clothing, and everything that is going on. Sometimes the environment just does not lend itself to group travel. Those you take on a trip must be trusted. You don't have time to teach them how to pray with you; they must be at that maturity level before getting on the airplane.

I know there are times when you can take people with you, but you must go into a distinctive environment. When we take groups overseas, we go first and scout the proposed areas. Some may be rustic and dangerous. For example, I couldn't tell you how many times I have had to preach with armed guards standing on both ends of the stage. They don't make a point of flashing their guns, but they are there because some places are far from safe.

It is not wise to take an infant in the Lord to that kind of place; it's not wise for them or you. Paul is dealing with this type of environment. Barnabas wanted to take someone that Paul did not feel was ready for where they were going. Look back at this passage:

> But Paul thought not good to take him with them, who departed from them from Pamphylia, and went not with them to the work. And the contention was so sharp between them, that they departed asunder one from the other: and so Barnabas took Mark, and sailed unto Cyprus; And Paul chose Silas, and departed, being recommended by the brethren unto the grace of God. And he went through Syria and Cilicia, confirming the churches (Acts 15:38-41).

We don't know who the head of this team was. Barnabas was originally in the lead when he initially took Paul to introduce him to the other apostles. However, by functional authority—how it works when you get on the field—Paul seems to have emerged as the leader. That was evidenced by the fact that Paul wrote half the New Testament, and Barnabas wrote none. The functional leader was Paul.

You can see the progression happening here. Barnabas was the initial leader, and he introduced Paul. In Acts 13, Both men operated as a prophet and teacher. After going through their preparation and schooling, they separated for the real work. At this point, they needed the endorsement of the body of Christians.

The Bible does not say they just went on a road trip; no, they were sent out. Some people just go. It never works spiritually when you just go; it only works when you are sent. Anybody can call you, but only one group can send you, and those are the ones who know you. Only those who know you can vouch for you. The Bible says to, "know them which labour among you" (1 Thessalonians 5:12).

After a time, the contention about John Mark grew between Paul and Barnabas to such a sharp point that they had to separate from each other. What's interesting is that after this event, Barnabas was never mentioned again in the New Testament. Barnabas walked out of his destiny, never to recover it again.

PARTNERSHIP OF COOPERATION

There is a place for you with people who have been put in your life on purpose. If you do not treat those relationships well, you will walk out of your destiny and never experience it. You can go to heaven, you can have some degree of Christian success, you can love God with all your heart, but you will not get done what you were put here to do. There will always be a missing ingredient—something that should have been there that wasn't—because you did not honor the relationships the Lord gave you. Not every person who comes into your life is necessarily a person of destiny for you, but some are.

Strife brings confusion, so you cannot recognize who they are if there is strife. And, if you cannot recognize the people of destiny in your life, how are you going to know who they are? Sometimes you can't identify them on the front end; it becomes an unfolding process, and you see the compatibility. You begin to see things, and you gather things about the other person working with you. You must know who they are.

To grow in God, you will grow by the Word, but you will often grow much more when God introduces you to someone who knows Him better than you do. Why? Because they walk in the Word and aspects of God where you have yet to walk. God ties you together with these people to mature you and bring you up a level or two. If you avoid the connection, you won't get the input you need to take you to your next step. It would be like taking an algebra or calculus class before becoming proficient in basic math. There is going to be a lot of homework. That is the way our life is in God. We need to learn the basics before obtaining an advanced degree; we need to be ready. We must prepare ourselves to receive it.

You have a "lot" that God gives you, but it takes a partnership of cooperation. You need to know what that is and that it is unfolding in nature. Some of it you know in the beginning, and then some things unfold in your life just as it did with Paul and Barnabas. God is going to bring people into your life, and they are there for good reason.

Paul wrote half of the New Testament, but Barnabas walked out of his destiny for good. Paul was right, and Barnabas was not. I am talking about the functional authority that is implied in Scripture. Then Silas, who listened to the Holy Ghost and stayed strong and in place, stepped into his destiny. Destiny can be changed; God will only put up with us being out of place for so long. Some think, *"If I don't do it, it won't get done."* Wrong. God will use someone else.

God's plan was completed, but Barnabas did not do it. Fact: The will of God will be done. Barnabas stepped out of his destiny, and Silas stepped in. Destiny is cooperative—a partnership between you and the Lord. God begins to reveal things, but we must honor them.

When we believe that we do not need others or fail to honor divine relationships by allowing strife to rule us, we are most certainly taking a step out of our destiny. There is not just a place for you to be, there are relationships that must be honored before you fulfill your destiny. By the way, God will test you with relationships. You may say, *"God doesn't test us."* You're about half right; God does not test us with evil, but He does test our hearts. You can count on that.

Our decisions must cooperate with our destiny and not move us away but draw us close. Barnabas walked away while Paul stayed in his destiny. Just like Abraham said to Lot, *"Let there be no strife, I pray thee, between me and thee."* Not even a little bit. None.

9
HONORING RELATIONSHIPS

Paul said this in 1 Corinthians:

> Am I am not an apostle? am I not free? have I
> not seen Jesus Christ our Lord? are not ye my
> work in the Lord? If I be not an apostle unto
> others, yet doubtless I am to you: for the seal of
> mine apostleship are ye in the Lord (1
> Corinthians 9:1-2).

Of course, those are rhetorical questions that are answered with
an absolute "yes." Yes, he is an apostle. Yes, he saw the Lord.
There are people that God will bring into your life, who may
not be an apostle to everyone, but God may use them to
minister to you in a unique way. I am not a pastor to everyone,
but I am the pastor at my church.

You cannot have two pastors. That is the nature of a pastoral
relationship. If a man asked his wife if he could bring another
woman home, how would she feel? For a marriage covenant
relationship to work, there must be two people agreeing to the
terms. Loyalty requires focus, or it is not loyalty.

COOPERATING WITH YOUR DESTINY

"Well, I can listen to any pastor," you say. I am not saying you can't listen to other pastors. However, I am saying that when God unites your heart with someone, it becomes a non-negotiable relationship. You must receive your pastor with the honor that God intended for it to have. Relationships are not one-way propositions. For a pastoral covenant to work, there also must be two people agreeing to the covenant terms.

When correction comes from a spiritual authority, there has to be this thing in the body that causes us to grow up and not be so inflamed. I will be the first one to tell you that I need lots of improvement. I need to grow just like everyone else, so I am willing to listen to correction. We can't be a law unto ourselves. I am not perfect, and I make mistakes. We all make mistakes, and so we all need to be correctable. Allow the Word of God to be your final authority and live by it. There needs to be some give and take by recognizing divine relationships in your life.

Relationships must be honored, they must be esteemed. Sometimes we mess up, but we want to avoid that as much as possible.

ALL PARTS OF THE BODY ARE IMPORTANT

The Bible talks about how the body needs all the parts:

> For the body is not one member, but many. **If the foot shall say, Because I am not the hand, I am not of the body; is it therefore not of the body?** And if the ear shall say, Because I am not the eye, I am not of the body; is it therefore not of the body? If the whole body were an eye, where were the hearing? If the whole were

> hearing, where were the smelling? But now
> hath God set the members every one of them
> in the body, as it hath pleased him (1
> Corinthians 12:14-18, emphasis added).

Hold up your hand and look at your index finger. If that finger was severed from the hand, the finger would eventually die unless it was reattached some way. The hand would continue to live, albeit handicapped because it is still attached to the body, but the finger would not live. So, the hand cannot say to the finger, *"I don't need you,"* and the finger cannot say to the hand, *"I don't need you."* That is what He said. That's the give and take part of the relationship. Paul referred to us as the "body of Christ, and members in particular" (1 Corinthians 12:27). The forearm cannot say to the upper arm, *"I don't need you."* The hand sure cannot say to the forearm, *"I don't need you."* He went on to expand this truth in Ephesians:

> From whom the whole body fitly joined
> together and compacted by that which every
> joint supplieth, according to the effectual
> working in the measure of every part, maketh
> increase of the body unto the edifying of itself
> in love (Ephesians 4:16).

Notice it says that the body is edified by the joint. What does that mean? The finger is edified because it is joined. You break the joining, and it loses its life. The Bible says every joint supplies, so when you break your joint from that destined relationship, you cut off your spiritual supply.

One might say, *"I can do this anyway."* No, you cannot. There is a supply in the spirit that must be maintained, and if you don't, there is an element you will always be missing. I am not saying that there is just one supply of the spirit. Different people supply different things. However, there are ordained relationships that you must recognize as part of your destiny, and the supply is critical to your future. The word "supply" means contribution and nourishment; it means to add, furnish, and minister. Every **joint** where you are connected becomes your supply. We should all realize who these people are in our lives.

KING DAVID

King David had many sons, but we'll look at two in particular: Solomon and Absalom. According to Scripture, Solomon honored his relationship with his father and became the wisest and wealthiest man on earth. God used him to build the greatest temple—possibly the most remarkable, most opulent, and most spectacular building ever built. That is what honoring a relationship will do.

Absalom *dis*honored his relationship with his father, and it caused him a premature death and unending ridicule. Thousands of years later, we talk about him as a traitor and a betrayer exiled from his home. These are two boys from the same father, with the glaring exception that one honored the relationship, and one did not.

RUTH AND NAOMI

In the story of Ruth and Naomi, we see that Naomi's husband and two sons died. Following the deaths, one son's wife, Orpha, chose to go back to the gods of her native homeland. However, her other daughter-in-law, Ruth, told Naomi:

> But Ruth replied, "Don't make me leave you, for I want to go wherever you go and to live wherever you live; your people shall be my people, and your God shall be my God; I want to die where you die and be buried there. May the Lord do terrible things to me if I allow anything but death to separate us" (Ruth 1:16-17).

We read about Ruth in the lineage of the Savior because she honored a relationship. Her whole life began to take on the destiny that God intended because she recognized that Naomi was part of her future, and she would not give it up, no matter what. Again, not all relationships have destiny, but some do, and we must recognize the difference.

HONORING JESUS

> And when [Jesus] was come near, he beheld the city, and wept over it, Saying, If thou hadst known, even thou, at least in this thy day, the things which belong unto thy peace! but now they are hid from thine eyes. For the days shall come upon thee, that thine enemies shall cast a trench about thee, and compass thee round, and keep thee in on every side, And shall lay thee even with the ground, and thy children within thee; and they shall not leave in thee one stone upon another; **because** thou knewest not the time of thy visitation (Luke 19:41-44, emphasis added).

In this passage, Jesus foretells the future of Jerusalem. **"Because"** is the connecting word in this passage and identifies their failure. Jesus was saying, *"You did not recognize who I was and what I brought to you and the relationship that God was bringing to you through Me."*

Because they did not recognize Him, they did not fulfill their destiny. If we are going to fulfill our destiny, the number one relationship we must recognize is Jesus Christ. We must be true to Him.

As we honor God, He will bring people into our lives for various purposes. People are not always kind, but you can't control that; you are the only one you can control. You have to be kind, even if it is not reciprocated or even acknowledged. There will be people deposited in your life to teach you the Word of God, and you will never have a close relationship with them. That's okay if you recognize what role they play. There are people I listen to from a distance because they feed me. I may not know them personally, but I know them by the Spirit. God will bring special people into our lives—special relationships that require us to treat them honorably, with dignity, and with the respect they deserve.

10

PRESSING THROUGH THE DARKNESS

Let's look at the story of Abraham's walk with God as it continues to unfold.

> After these things the word of the Lord came unto Abram in a vision, saying, Fear not, Abram: I am thy shield, and thy exceeding great reward. And Abram said, Lord God, what wilt thou give me, seeing I go childless, and the steward of my house is this Eliezer of Damascus? (Genesis 15:1-2).

Here we begin to glimpse Abraham's dilemma—the internal challenges he was facing with God. God told him his seed would be as the dust, and a great nation would come from him. That was a promise from God, and he heard it accurately.

Sometimes we can hear the Lord's voice, but after a season of time, we may question, *"Lord, will this ever happen?"* The things of life: trials, challenges, troubles, difficulties, and delays can cause us all to begin to question if you heard the Lord in the first place. *"Lord, was I listening close enough to understand you accurately? Was that Your voice, Lord, or did I miss it? Am I moving in the right direction?"*

After receiving God's promise, Abraham continued to move in God. His question in this verse is not speaking from a rebellious heart; He is still walking with the Lord.

Later we find that Abraham's faith in the Lord was counted to him as righteousness or right standing in the economy of God. Let's look at two translations of this truth:

> "And Abram believed God; then God considered
> him righteous on account of his faith"
> (Genesis 15:6, TLB).

> "Abram believed the Lord. And the Lord
> accepted Abram's faith, and that faith made
> him right with God" (Genesis 15:6, NCV).

In Genesis 15, Abraham did not question God due to lost faith; however, he was beginning to question whether he had actually heard and understood God. With the delay in fulfillment of God's promise, the darkness around Abraham caused him to wonder, and he asked the question, *"Lord, what will You give me?"*

The promise of the Lord to Abraham said, *"I will make you a great nation. Your offspring shall be as the dust of the earth."* That covenant promise was really for someone else—us! He was referring to his heritage and all those that came after him, which includes us.

In the midst of the battle over Lot's captivity and all the other trials that came, Abraham questioned God by saying, *"What about me? I am a part of this equation, too. I am going to follow you; I am going to obey you. But what about me? Don't forget me."*

There are promises for your future that God wants to do with you and your fruitfulness. When you get separated by darkness and delay from what you **do**, you must deal with who you **are**, which is often a dramatic difference.

Abraham wondered, *"What about me?"* That is not a self-centered person asking a selfish question. That is a person who is walking with God asking a legitimate question. When the darkness of life was all around, and the delays were ever-present, Abraham asked this simple question—just like you and I would ask.

We are talking about walking in your destiny. There are times when we all may question God. When it appears like the promises you heard and the things that you believe the Lord said to you seem so distant and far away—like they could or would never happen—we may question God. At times like that, the reality may be: *"I want to know about the great and wonderful things that You are doing in others. I want to know prophetic Scripture. I want to know about this and that. But what about me?"*

You have a Savior who cares about you personally. I thank God that Jesus died for the sins of the world, but I also thank God that Jesus died for my sins, too.

Sometimes we get it all caught up in the big picture and lose our identity. And that is what Abraham is saying, *"What about me?"* It is not a selfish question. It's an important question—one that we all ask if we are honest because, after all, we do want to know the answer to it.

GOD'S REASSURANCE

Abraham questioned, *"Lord, what will you give me, seeing I go childless?"* He had the promise of his seed, but he said, I don't even have a child. He had one delay after another. Delay, delay, delay. *"I don't even have a child. How could you possibly do what You said You would do? Did I hear you right? Was I mistaken? Will it ever happen?"* He must have given it a lot of thought to ask if his heir would be his servant, Eliezer. Was he supposed to adopt Eliezer? The Lord had to intervene to give Abraham some clarity.

You need to understand that when we get into our dark time, our questioning time, God needs to speak to us, and we need to listen. Let's look at these verses in context:

> After these things the word of the Lord came unto Abram in a vision, saying, Fear not, Abram: I am thy shield, and thy exceeding great reward. And Abram said, Lord God, what wilt thou give me, seeing I go childless, and the steward of my house is this Eliezer of Damascus? And Abram said, Behold, to me thou hast given no seed: and, lo, one born in my house is mine heir. And, behold, the word of the Lord came unto him, saying, This shall not be thine heir; but he that shall come forth out of thine own bowels shall be thine heir (Genesis 15:1-4).

The word of the Lord came to him in his dark moment when his destiny was all but gone. Delays had become too lengthy and numerous, and too many mornings had provided him with the absence of change. No change. Just like you and I might experience.

The Lord stopped him and corrected him. God said Abraham's heir was not coming from the outside but from the inside. He said, *"The heir I promised you—this great nation I promised you—is going to come out of your loins. It is going to come from the inside of you."*

In our deep, dark, questioning moments, God comes to provide reassurance to us.

And he brought him forth abroad, and said,
Look now toward heaven, and tell the stars, if
thou be able to number them: and he said unto
him, So shall thy seed be (Genesis 15:5).

Here we have God speaking again about Abraham's seed. The first time the Lord spoke to him about his offspring, He said, "I will make thy seed as the dust" (Genesis 13:16). Now God speaks to him again and says that his seed would be as the stars. He was saying:

Abram, at midnight, when you're out of hope and can't find anyone to encourage you—just go and look up at the sky. That's all it will take because the stars will be there to testify of what I am going to do with you and what I have intended for you.

APPLICATION FOR TODAY

That's the way it is with us. God comes to us with a reminder. Now, it is interesting that God uses the dust that is born of clay in this illustration. Adam was made of dust, and God breathed into him. We also see in the Bible that those who turn many to righteousness shall shine as the stars forever. God is saying to Abraham that what starts in the dust and dirt, He has destined for an eternity beyond the stars. That is your life.

Your life may well have started in the dirt or gutter. It may have begun on the "wrong side of the tracks" while staring hopelessness in the eye. It may have started with parents who cared little about you and believed you were nothing but a mistake. That sounds bleak but hang on a minute; God said that in Him, you are going to end up beyond the stars. That is God's destiny for you. Just remember, when you wonder about things and find yourself a bit confused, go out into the night and look up and see those stars. That is what God has intended. And not just for Abraham, either, because the blessings of Abraham have come on us through Christ Jesus (Galatians 3:14).

God has a destiny for you that is so far beyond anything you could ask, think, or imagine. It has not entered into the mind or heart of man, the things God has prepared for those who love Him and walk with Him. You have a destiny that is much greater than you could have ever planned for yourself. And that is what God intends for you.

He takes the dust and turns it into the stars. He takes the dirtiest of the dirty and causes it to glisten like a jewel. That is what Jesus does for us.

And he brought him forth abroad, and said,
Look now toward heaven, and tell the stars, if
thou be able to number them: and he said unto
him, So shall thy seed be. And he believed in
the Lord; and he counted it to him for
righteousness. And he said unto him, I am the
Lord that brought thee out of Ur of the
Chaldees, to give thee this land to inherit it.
And he said, Lord God, whereby shall I know
that I shall inherit it? (Genesis 15:5-8).

Abraham asked two important questions. First, Lord, what will
you give me? Second, how shall I know it? In other words,
Abraham needed some validation. He needed for God to create
some circumstances around him that confirmed what he was
hearing.

Sometimes you need validation. You need things in your life to
tell you that you are marching lockstep with God, in sequence
and harmony with Him. You need circumstances to match up
with what has been spoken to your heart. You need God to
create some events to let you know—just like Abraham needed
to know.

"How am I going to know?" It was not a question of doubt
because we see in the verse above it, Abraham believed God;
there was not a doubt. This question says, *"I need You to confirm
this to me. Let me see. Let me understand."*

It's at times like this when we talk to God about the realities of
our life. This is where all phoniness is laid aside. This is when
we get down to who we really are and who God is to us. This
is where we come to terms with the reality of what we are put

here to do and what we are put here to become. We may want to pray something like this:

> *Lord, what will You give me, and how am I going to know it? Give me a legitimate way to know. I need assurance that I am truly following Your plan. Let me know that I am not moving in human emotion. Let me know that I am not just wasting my life on impossible dreams.*

It does not do us any good to dream if the dream didn't come from the Lord. To dream any dream that God did not inspire is just a daydream.

In pursuing our destiny, we will all experience times when we need the Lord's reassurance and His confirmation. We need to press into the darkness and through the dark times. Notice that the Lord did not get angry or upset with these questions. He will not get angry with you, either. As a matter of fact, sometimes He is waiting for this type of question.

Some may respond, *"Well, I'm moving in faith; I wouldn't dare to upset the Lord with questions."* It is your life; you just get one pass at it. I talk to God about all of it. It won't bother Him. The Lord never gets upset when we inquire of Him. What does upset the Lord is failing to inquire of Him, pursuing false voices, or following self-will.

We must keep the voice of the flesh somewhere else. Abraham listened to his wife's fear, and we are still living off that one today with that Hagar and Ishmael incident. That one is in the news every day; I'll leave that for you to research.

A LIFE-LONG JOURNEY

God began to confirm His word to Abraham when the promise was delayed. Abraham received these promises from the Lord at 75 years old, but He was nearing 100 when the heir was born. There was a significant delay for God's promise to come to pass.

When we get a word from the Lord, we think it's going to happen tomorrow. He gives you a word for your life, and we add it to our calendar for tomorrow before noon. God gives you a word to direct the rest of your life on this planet.

That's why I have a little problem with all this casual *"God told me this"* and *"God told me that"* business. If God really tells you something, it will put you on a life-long journey. I am not saying that God does or does not speak regularly. What I am talking about is when people go around claiming, *"I heard from God about this and about that."* If you really hear from God, it will direct your entire life. It is highly improbable that God will give you an inspired word on what restaurant to go to or what movie to see. God wants to give you a word that directs your entire eternity.

I am not saying He won't give you mid-course corrections, but I am talking about a word. Sometimes I think we are too casual about that. I know the Holy Spirit is always speaking, and you can undoubtedly get impressions from the Lord. However, every word and every impression will be consistent with the main word He has spoken for your life. God is not confused.

People are conditioned to want updates and changes. We hear ourselves praying, *"Lord, I know you spoke that to me, but don't you understand that's going to be difficult for me to do. Do you have anything else up there? How about another word?"* Then we try to help Him accomplish it by the arm of the flesh—big mistake. Your destiny cannot be fulfilled apart from God, so every time you begin to step out of His plan for your life, you begin to cast your own lot.

Remember, the word "lot" is the root word for **lottery.** That's when you begin to play the luck game with your future rather than obeying God for the outcome. When you start to play the game of chance, game of luck, and rolling the dice for your future, you will not like where it takes you. Alternatively, you will love where God takes you if you are willing to do it His way and obey what He says.

"Well, I believe you can be anything you want to be." Sounds good, but I don't believe that at all. I believe God has a plan for you, and I believe you can precisely be what He called you and created you to be.

I can tell you this: He did call you and create you for more than you realize is possible. He has a plan for you that is greater than the one you would have designed for yourself. If you are willing to follow Him, He will take you from the dust to the stars.

You Must Stop the Enemy

I want to call your attention to the part of Abraham's story when God showed him the stars, and in response, Abraham made a sacrifice to the Lord. Notice this verse again:

> "And when the fowls came down upon the carcases, Abram drove them away" (Genesis 15:11).

Jesus taught the Parable of the Sower in Mark, chapter 4, which says that the sower sows the Word, and a plant grows up; the fowls come and dwell in the branches, the shadows, and the shade.

When you find fowls of the air, it represents demonic activity in almost every case. Notice Abraham's cycle here: He heard a word from the Lord, made a sacrifice to the Lord, and the devil immediately came in the form of the fowls of the air.

But notice: God did not run the devil off; instead, it says Abraham ran him off. When confusion or delay comes—or anything that besets you—you are responsible for taking care of it yourself; satan will not stop until you stop him. You might say, *"I'm believing for God to stop him."* Sorry, He is not going to do it.

Remember, getting rid of the enemy is a cooperative endeavor. God gave us His name to go into all the world and cast out the devil. If we don't cast him out, he is not leaving.

Someone might reply, *"Well, I prayed for God to cast him out."* In that case, we are praying about what God has already given us the authority to do; we should avoid that. A Christian may want the Lord to get the devil off their back, but God answers, *"Okay. Use My name, and he will flee."* But we want to do everything besides what He told us to do. We want Him to send us the intercessory team. We want Him to give us a sign from heaven. However, His response is, *"No, you stop the devil. If you don't stop him, he won't stop."*

Abraham made this sacrifice to the Lord in honor of God's promise. Satan came immediately, and Abraham had to drive him away. Let's look at the next verse:

"And when the sun was going down, a deep
sleep fell upon Abram; and, lo, an horror of
great darkness fell upon him" (Genesis 15:12).

This verse demonstrates why we must press through the darkness. The Bible says, "an horror of great darkness fell upon him." In modern vernacular, Abram was having a panic attack. The fear of failure, the fear of not getting to where he needed to be, the fear of thinking he was "losing it"—not really hearing God's voice, the torment of doubt, can be the horror that is often attached to being a man or a woman led by the Spirit of God. You step out in faith, and no one understands; you do something, but no one knows what it feels like. When you think you are absolutely, utterly alone that the penetrating darkness begins to surround you. It's what you do at times like this that determines whether you fulfill your destiny or give it up for some other offer.

Maybe you feel misunderstood or betrayed. I'm with you on that one. I know what it is to help people, and then those very people are the ones who stab you in the back. I know that feeling. I know what it feels like when people turn against you for no reason or justification. However, those things do not change anything I am doing. You have to become determined to finish your course. With God's help, you are going to do this. You need to be determined in the dark times.

Misunderstanding has nothing to do with it. Wanting everyone's approval has nothing to do with it. No one has ever done significant things in the Kingdom and received the absolute approval of all the bystanders. Everyone believes in you after you do something, but nobody will help you in the beginning.

WE ARE ALL INTER-CONNECTED

Let's read this again about the great horror coming on Abram:

> And when the sun was going down, a deep
> sleep fell upon Abram; and, lo, an horror of
> great darkness fell upon him. And he said unto
> Abram, Know of a surety that thy seed shall be
> a stranger in a land that is not theirs, and shall
> serve them; and they shall afflict them four
> hundred years; (Genesis 15:12-13).

God was trying to give Abraham some perspective. It was
going to take 400 years before his seed would come out of
captivity. Abraham wanted the word God gave him to happen
immediately. But God said:

> *No, Abraham, it's going to take at least four
> hundred years of captivity that have to be
> worked through before you see the promise. You
> are investing in a destiny that is not going to
> be completed with you; it will be completed by
> a group coming centuries after you.*

Remember, child of God, our lives are interconnected, and
your life is not your own. Your life is not just yours to live; it
affects and touches a vast number of others. The destiny that
God gives you has eternal consequences in the lives of
multitudes of others. If we selfishly think that it is about us and
our fulfillment alone, we have not thought it through. The
fulfillment of your destiny in God is not just about you,
individually; it is about much more than you.

God had to give Abraham some perspective. Yes, remarkable things are coming. Yes, there is a future. Yes, there is a hope. Yes, there is a destiny. Yes, there is something great. Yes, the dust is going to become like the stars. However, there are 400 years of captivity before much of it will be seen. Perspective gave Abram some peace so he could make his trek through life with the necessary joy to see things through. Abram had to be okay with knowing that all of it wasn't going to happen tomorrow.

Your life is hidden for an eternal reason, and you cannot judge it before it is time. You must sow while considering eternity—not the short term of next week or next month.

LIVING WITH ETERNITY IN MIND

Abraham did ask God some fair questions: What about me and how will I know it? Those are legitimate questions in the scope of his journey. God didn't take him beyond that, but He did mention the 400 years. He is focusing Abraham on the future that he will not see. The Lord goes on to say that there will be a stranger in the land:

> And he said unto Abram, Know of a surety that thy seed shall be a stranger in a land that is not theirs, and shall serve them; and they shall afflict them four hundred years; And also that nation, whom they shall serve, will I judge: and afterward shall they come out with great substance. And thou shalt go to thy fathers in peace; thou shalt be buried in a good old age (Genesis 15:13-15).

Pressing Through the Darkness

This is my translation of what God was saying:

> *What I am doing with you will not all be seen in your lifetime. It is not going to impact just you; this is a whole lot bigger than one person. What I do in you is going to affect multitudes. I want you to know that I have you right here in the palm of my hand. You are going to fulfill your days, and you are going to live a long and productive life.*

Abram received this call when he was at the tender young age of 75; he died at 175. Abram did not know that most of his life was still ahead of him as he questioned the Lord. He thought his life was almost at the end, but there was more to be lived.

Sometimes we measure our lives by how much has gone by, while God measures by how much is ahead. God fulfilled Abraham in a spectacular, tremendous way, making him one of the richest men in that part of the world. When God spoke, Abraham trusted Him, and He eventually gave him many offspring, but there was no child from his loins for many years. The fulfillment was still on the horizon.

What do you do when you press into the dark? Are you full of doubt? Do you give up? Do you look back? Do you quit? Do you think it is never going to happen? Is it taking too long? We need to remember that we are to live our lives with the scope of eternity in front of us.

Abram was shortsighted. At 75, he had no idea that he had another hundred years left. Then God shared His promise with him: you will have a peaceful life and die at a good, old age. Your life will not be cut short before it is time.

You may think you are over the hill, but with a word from the Lord, you just may be getting started. God is building for eternity, and He can keep you here as long as He needs you.

JOHN THE BAPTIST IN THE DARK TIMES

Looking at John the Baptist, we know Scripture speaks much praise of this man of God. Of his contemporaries, he was the closest to Jesus. They were born near the same time, and John the Baptist baptized Jesus. Because of some particular events, John found himself in prison. But in that dark time, just before he was beheaded, Luke tells us that John the Baptist sent one of his friends to Jesus to ask Him, *"Are you the one, or do we look for another?"* Jesus sent word back to him with His answer, *"Tell him the blind see, and the crippled walk."*

When the dark times come, we may doubt everything. When the difficulties come, we question, *"Lord, did I hear You? Was it really You that spoke to me?"* Jesus sent John the Baptist a reminder of who He was.

MOSES IN THE DARK TIMES

And then there was Moses. He was raised in the palace of the king and groomed for leadership. At forty years old, the Scripture says he knew what he was called to do. He knew his purpose but tried to make things happen through the arm of the flesh, which got him into trouble. He had to flee for his life and was exiled to the desert. While tending sheep on the backside of the desert, the Bible says God spoke to Moses.

Here we have a man who knew what he was called to do, but all hope was gone. He had forty years of tending sheep while knowing he was called to lead the children of Israel. At that time, God came to him in the form of a burning bush and began to speak to him, but Moses did not want to do it. Finally, he did respond appropriately.

Following his exile of forty years or half of his life, God began to renew what Moses initially heard and gave more definition to it. He said, *"I want you to go down to Egypt and tell Pharaoh to let my people go."* Moses' response was, *"I can't speak, Lord."* So, God told him to take Aaron and let him speak. With that, Moses followed God.

With what had become dust in his life, at 120 years old, Moses was leading the children of Israel. For 40 years, he was agonizing with a desire to go on into the Promised Land. The man that had completely given up any hope of destiny in God, suddenly, at 120, was begging God for the opportunity to do it but one more day.

That is when you go from the dust to the stars. God has a destiny for you that will take you from the ash heap to the palace. I believe it with all my heart.

NOAH PRESSED ON IN THE DARK TIMES

The man Noah got a word from the Lord to build a boat, which would ultimately save the entire human race. A hundred years later, he was ridiculed and misunderstood because he built an ark in the middle of the desert, where it had never yet rained! Can you imagine what they were saying about Noah? But the Scripture says he was a preacher of righteousness. He never quit preaching the truths of God. To Noah, He was the God of Glory.

Noah never quit; he always held to his faith. By his demonstration of obedience to the Lord—in the face of ridicule and misunderstanding with an unwillingness to stop and give in—Noah stepped into his destiny. With that, he is recorded as one of the heroes of faith (Hebrews 11) and one of the greatest figures in the entire Bible. We will know him throughout eternity because he is one of our brothers in Christ.

Noah reached his destiny because he refused to quit in the dark times. In the face of misunderstanding, he refused to relent. You must recognize that to realize your destiny in God, as did Noah, you have no choice but to press on.

DON'T JUDGE IT YET

The Apostle Paul said, "Therefore judge nothing before the time, until the Lord come" (1 Corinthians 4:5). You can judge your life by today's events, but you must ultimately base it on what eternity says. For you to realize your destiny, you must sow it for eternity, not just for the moment. You are building with a future that's far more than your children and grandchildren; you establish a future that has eternal significance. We must build with the big picture of eternity in mind. We need to press through the dark times and keep the fowls out. Your life counts because you have a destiny. Believe it, and it will come to pass.

I want to share a quote by Edwin Markham that is significant to me. This verse would be something worthy to commit to memory:

Ah! Great it is to believe the dream as we
stand in youth by the starry stream.

But a greater thing is to fight life through
and say at the end, the dream is true.

It is essential that you push through. God cannot take you to
where He wants you if you are a quitter. You must press
through the darkness.

COOPERATING WITH YOUR DESTINY

11
LISTEN TO RIGHT VOICES

Scripture identifies Abraham as the father of our faith. The things that happened to him happened not only for his profit but for our benefit also. As Christians, we are to follow the faith of Abraham. If Abraham is to be our example, then we would be wise to follow his faith.

Sometimes we see where he missed it and got off track, but he didn't stay there long; he got right back on the right path. He fulfilled the plan, purpose, and will of God for his life, but not without problems and mistakes.

Let's look at this passage from Genesis in context, and then we'll dissect it:

> Now Sarai Abram's wife bare him no children: and she had an handmaid, an Egyptian, whose name was Hagar. And Sarai said unto Abram, Behold now, the Lord hath restrained me from bearing: I pray thee, go in unto my maid; it may be that I may obtain children by her. And Abram hearkened to the voice of Sarai. And Sarai Abram's wife took Hagar her maid the Egyptian, after Abram had dwelt ten years in

the land of Canaan, and gave her to her husband Abram to be his wife. And he went in unto Hagar, and she conceived: and when she saw that she had conceived, her mistress was despised in her eyes. And Sarai said unto Abram, My wrong be upon thee: I have given my maid into thy bosom; and when she saw that she had conceived, I was despised in her eyes: the Lord judge between me and thee. But Abram said unto Sarai, Behold, thy maid is in thine hand; do to her as it pleaseth thee. And when Sarai dealt hardly with her, she fled from her face (Genesis 16:1-6).

There is a story that goes into greater detail than in these verses. It is important to note that in the day and the culture in which this event took place, having multiple wives was not considered immoral; it was common for men to have several wives. Since Sarah had not conceived, it would have been customary in that setting for her to take Hagar's child as her own. Understanding that tradition is important to us as we study.

The foundation has been clearly established that the Lord told Abraham that He was going to make his seed as the dust of the earth and the stars of the sky. There are two branches exemplified in Abraham's seed. The first is the seed that comes out of the dust or earth—Israel. The second is a spiritual seed, which represents you and me. We are not covenanted to the land as the Jewish people, but we are covenanted to God through the new birth. So, we become that spiritual seed that is represented by the stars.

There is a dual aspect or application to that delivery of God's covenant to His people: one being the chosen people, the Jews, and the other being the chosen people called the church. They are both important and significant.

God told Abraham, *"I am going to bring the covenant blessing on you and your seed after you."* When he was 75, he left his family's care to journey to the place God called him.

If you remember, we studied that there was a place of blessing. When they arrived at that place, Abram went on further. God had to work to get him back to the right place because it was a significant location. The blessing could not happen just anywhere; it had to happen in the right place.

At this time, Abraham and Sarah are obviously getting older, and Sarah has never conceived a child. Due to the worry and anxiety of starting a family, this couple went down a path that many of us might be prone to go. They decided to help God do what He promised even though it was His responsibility to fulfill it.

> In the same day the Lord made a covenant with Abram, saying, Unto thy seed have I given this land, from the river of Egypt unto the great river, the river Euphrates: (Genesis 15:18).

From this verse, you can clearly see that God made a covenant with Abraham and gave his seed the land. This agreement is in the form of a covenant—a binding word.

Then, human reasoning begins to set in. The realities of the flesh start to settle in, and Sarah begins to wonder if she will ever conceive. *"It hasn't happened yet. Will it ever? Can it ever be?"* Look at this passage of Scripture again:

> Now Sarai Abram's wife bare him no children: and she had an handmaid, an Egyptian, whose name was Hagar. And Sarai said unto Abram, Behold now, the Lord hath restrained me from bearing: I pray thee, go in unto my maid; it may be that I may obtain children by her. **And Abram hearkened to the voice of Sarai** (Genesis 16:1-2, emphasis added).

Abraham listened to Sarah. There isn't anything wrong with men listening and paying attention to what their wives have to say. In fact, later in the story, the Bible says that God's blessing came on Abraham because he listened to his wife. In this case, however, the problem began when he listened to his wife instead of listening to the Lord.

A voice speaks in Abraham's life that takes him away from His covenant with God. At that point, God did not intervene or offer instruction. If you will remember, a chapter before, Abraham had just asked if his heir would be his servant Eleazar? God reassured him that his heir would not be Eleazar or anyone close to him, but it would be someone who comes out of him.

For some reason, we feel compelled to help God fulfill His Word. Since Sarah is barren, they decided to use Hagar as a substitute. Hagar becomes pregnant, and God speaks to her about her son, who will be called Ishmael. We can see it unfold:

"From this pregnancy, you'll get a son: Name him Ishmael; for God heard you, God answered you. He'll be a bucking bronco of a man, a real fighter, fighting and being fought, always stirring up trouble, always at odds with his family" (Genesis 16:11-12, MSG).

However, God's covenant was with Abraham, and He told Abraham that their covenant would come through his son Isaac. Ishmael was a substitute or a false direction—another plan that came out of Abraham's loins that causes tremendous problems from that day until this. You have the devastation in Orlando, San Bernardino, Paris, and many other sites—ISIS (or ISIL) strikes violently around the world. This issues forth from the wild man, Ishmael, mentioned here, living out his desires throughout the earth today.

A False Plan

What took place with Ishmael was another plan, a diversion from the original. Can listening to the wrong voice get you in trouble? Can it usher in a substitute with a false plan? It pays to listen to the right voice. In this case, Ishmael, a product of the flesh, is produced by human beings trying to do for God what God intends to do Himself.

God covenants with you to bring a blessing; you have a destiny that He wants to fulfill in and through you. He wants to fulfill it for you, but also for Him; it is cooperative. You are a part of Him; He is a part of you. He said, *"My sheep hear my voice, and another they do not follow. Do it my way, and great blessings will come."*

119

If you listen to a false voice, it can put you in a ditch. The voice you give attention to will determine whether you fulfill God's destiny for your life. Remember, God has a destiny, but it is not automatic. I am convinced many voices are designed to take you out of God's plan for your life.

I have been a pastor for many years, so I have a great deal of experience, both personally and through people with whom I associate. Because of that, **I am convinced that listening to the wrong voice is the number one thing that takes people out of the plan of God for their lives.**

People live in a place of spiritual blessing and benefit; they are in a place where the supply of God is flowing. Then, another voice comes with a word. The people then become disgruntled, and dissatisfaction sets in, which morphs into faultfinding. Soon after that, they are looking at life from the front row of the ash heap. The ash heap happens when we try to do things out of the will of God. I have seen it so many times that I have stopped counting. It is such a common thing.

FAITH & PATIENCE

One of the ways to receive the blessing of God is through faith and patience. You inherit the promise by following this verse:

> "That ye be not slothful, but followers of them
> who **through faith and patience inherit the promises**"
> (Hebrews 6:12, emphasis added).

This verse does not say you inherit God's promises through struggling faith and agitated movements. In fact, if you are worried, you are not in God's will because you continue to struggle. You cannot be worried and anxious about fulfilling God's plan and remain in the will of God because worry and faith do not work together. You have a choice to make: stand in faith or quit. Choose to stand.

We listen to wrong voices and make bad decisions when we don't see how God could possibly fulfill His promise. Abraham did not see it all coming, either; it was not happening fast enough. He was one hundred years old, and Sarah was ninety when Isaac was born. They received their promise twenty-five years earlier. Twenty-five years had elapsed. As soon as they received the promise from God, the doubt settled in.

All the things that try to move us off track began to come in and interfere with Abraham and Sarah's faith. Words like: *"You know, I don't believe you even heard from God,"* or *"That word you got must not have been God,"* or *"Even if it was God you heard, He wants us to do our part."*

When you try to do it on your own or try through human reasoning to fulfill God's plan, you'll find yourself in trouble. The flesh, according to Scripture, is at enmity or hostile toward God. Ishmael was a product of the flesh, and Isaac was the seed of the spirit. Let's look at Romans:

> For to be carnally minded is death; but to be spiritually minded is life and peace. Because the carnal mind is enmity against God: for it is not subject to the law of God, neither indeed can be. So then they that are in the flesh cannot please God (Romans 8:6-8).

Here is the same passage in The Living Bible:

> Following after the Holy Spirit leads to life and
> peace, but following after the old nature leads to
> death because the old sinful nature within us is
> against God. It never did obey God's laws and
> it never will. That's why those who are still
> under the control of their old sinful selves, bent
> on following their old evil desires, can never
> please God (Romans 8:6-8, TLB).

Trying to function through the arm of the flesh will put you in
dire straits because human reasoning and rationalization can
take over. You can even put it down on paper and work out
why you should do something. Let me tell you this: don't lean
on the flesh. The sheep hear God's voice, and your life is better
when you go where the Good Shepherd tells you. He will help
you avoid heartache down that road. At first, it may look right,
but there is heartache coming straight at you with tragedy
settling in and sitting tall in the saddle. God has a destiny for
you, but you must do it His way, His place, and in His timing.
You must obey His voice.

Some may say, *"Well, I can't hear God's voice."* If you can't hear
His voice, why are you arguing with Him? You need to be
honest; you probably know precisely what He is telling you to
do because you are telling Him all the reasons why it won't
work. Failing to follow Him may get you some unwanted
results. Be careful; you don't want to have an Ishmael on your
hands. Ishmael is a type or example of disobedience to God; it
is a product of the flesh. Your flesh is in enmity—in direct
opposition—to God. It will always produce something that
God never intended.

Abraham got in trouble because he went ahead of God. He tried to undertake God's responsibility and refused to wait. He took matters into his own hands by listening to Sarah's voice. The words of the flesh were coming at him as a super train: *"You know, we're getting older every day. It is not going to happen if we wait. We have to make it happen."*

Your destiny is seen in the scope of eternity; it does not have to take place today. When God gives you a word, it is a word for life, not just for the moment. He very well may have some momentary things He wants you to do, but God's destiny is big, broad, and profound enough to take you on into forever.

If you understand you are building for eternity and not for the moment, it helps you overcome some of the challenges of the day. You will have challenges, but learn to enjoy life by changing your impatient and restless ways.

LIVING WITH THE CONSEQUENCES

Notice something about God in this whole event with Ishmael. Did you notice that He did not eliminate the circumstances of sowing to the flesh? Some of us want to obey our own will. We want to do it our own way, and then we want God to give us a crop failure. This problem did not go away; it is still living today. Hagar's hate for Sarah is what rules in the Middle East, and that hatred drives most terrorist activity today. God does not eliminate the consequence of our actions, and He does not eradicate the results, even though we really want Him to do it.

You may say, *"I didn't know; I made a mistake."* I know it's that way sometimes, but you still end up with Ishmael. At that point, it doesn't matter what you want to do; you have to deal with what you have. It's for reasons like this that we must take care to walk out our lives slowly. That is why we must be precise in our steps because we will get things we do not want. Then, we want God to deliver us from it, and it was not His doing. He will not deliver you from it, but He will help you in the middle of it.

Think about King David, who went up on the roof and looked where he should not have been looking. The Bible says it was the time of year when the king should be in battle, but David was on his rooftop fixated on Bathsheba. Because of that, he murdered the woman's husband and fathered a child that he should not have had.

The Scripture says because of King David's actions, a sword was brought into his household that never left, nor did its consequences. Yes, David was a man after God's own heart, but adultery was not part of the plan. However, it does mean that we have hope—even when we mess up. It does not mean that God writes you off forever, but the consequences do not evaporate.

Sometimes we want to act like there are no consequences; however, repercussions live on. We wonder why God allows it to continue, but we must understand the consequences are there because of what we did.

God is not the only eternal being. When you were born, you became one, too. And what you do has eternal consequences. Scripture says God breathed in us the breath of life. If you look that up in Hebrew, you see the word "life" as a plural. God breathed into us the breath of lives, which means we have the power to create and procreate, bringing life to things. When we bring life to things, they have eternal life in them, too.

God did not eliminate the consequences of Abraham's actions, nor did it change His original plan, but now we have to deal with Ishmael. God didn't need a Plan B; there was still going to be an Isaac. Having Ishmael did not stop God's plan.

God can give us Plan B's. If not, we would all be in trouble. God has a perfect will, but He also has an acceptable will and a good will. His perfect will is the best place to walk. However, if we had to be in the perfect will of God every time, no one would ever get anywhere. So, He does allow certain things, even though they may not be His best.

THE DEMISE OF KING SAUL

Think about the classic illustration when God called King Saul and gave him a destiny. He made Saul king over the nation of Israel. There is this idea that God called Saul, but then He changed His mind. Not so. God called Saul, and he messed it up. God knew what Saul would do, but He gave him a chance. God called King Saul with a destiny on his life.

I want you to look at a passage of Scripture where Saul had a call and destiny; he had a purpose in life. God set Saul up as king, but he reaped the consequences of doing things his own way.

> Now the Philistines fought against Israel; and the men of Israel fled from before the Philistines, and fell down slain in mount

125

Gilboa. And the Philistines followed hard after Saul, and after his sons; and the Philistines slew Jonathan, and Abinadab, and Malchishua, the sons of Saul. And the battle went sore against Saul, and the archers hit him, and he was wounded of the archers... So Saul died, and his three sons, and all his house died together... And it came to pass on the morrow, when the Philistines came to strip the slain, that they found Saul and his sons fallen in mount Gilboa. And when they had stripped him, they took his head, and his armour, and sent into the land of the Philistines round about, to carry tidings unto their idols, and to the people... So Saul died for his transgression which he committed against the Lord, even against the word of the Lord, which he kept not, and also for asking counsel of one that had a familiar spirit, to enquire of it; And enquired not of the Lord: therefore he slew him, and turned the kingdom unto David the son of Jesse (1 Chronicles 10:1-3, 6, 8-9, 13-14).

Saul had a destiny in God. He started out by removing those who were dealing in curious arts, witchcraft, and things of that nature, then he became fearful.

Now Samuel was dead, and all Israel had lamented him, and buried him in Ramah, even in his own city. And Saul had put away those that had familiar spirits, and the wizards, out of the land. And the Philistines gathered themselves together, and came and pitched in

Shunem: and Saul gathered all Israel together, and they pitched in Gilboa. And when Saul saw the host of the Philistines, **he was afraid,** and his heart greatly trembled (1 Samuel 28:3-5, emphasis added).

We can see here what fear will do. Fear will drive you in ways that you do not want to be driven. That is why I said worry is the opposite of faith. When you are in fear, you cannot move in faith. And here we find Saul moving in fear. Now, what happened is a result of moving in fear:

And when Saul enquired of the Lord, the Lord answered him not, neither by dreams, nor by Urim, nor by prophets. Then said Saul unto his servants, Seek me a woman that hath a familiar spirit (1 Samuel 28:6-7a).

Notice that you do not get a direct answer from God every time you call on Him. I surmise that Saul's disobedience probably had a lot to do with why God didn't respond. Saul was not exactly the model convert. He called on the Lord in this verse, and the Lord did not talk to him.

Here is Saul, the guy who ran off those with familiar spirits and the people who were moving in witchcraft and magic. He ran them out of town because those things were offensive to God. Then, his fear drove him to that very thing that offended the Lord.

Then said Saul unto his servants, **Seek me a woman that hath a familiar spirit, that I may go to her, and enquire of her.** And his servants said

> to him, Behold, there is a woman that hath a
> familiar spirit at Endor (1 Samuel 28:7,
> emphasis added).

This woman is often referred to as "the Witch of Endor." We find Saul here because he did not hear from God when and how he wanted. In the silence, Saul said, *"I am going to do this on my own. I am going to do it my way. I am going to get a word, and I am going to follow it."*

Fear drove Saul to seek a familiar spirit. He received direction for his future from the mouth of a witch; he definitely heard a voice that changed his life. We read where Samuel came back from the dead and made an appearance. Saul was a person who had to hear a voice. Even though they refuse to wait on God and listen to Him, some people still want a voice.

> "And Saul disguised himself, and put on other
> raiment, and he went..." (1 Samuel 28:8)

The king had already decreed that divination was against the law, and now he is sneaking around to visit a witch; that sounds like an internally conflicted human being. Saul was unwilling to wait on God to speak. In the same way that Abraham could not wait on God and sought another voice by listening to Sarah, Saul had to have a voice.

Saul is unable to hear the voice of the Lord, so he sought a familiar spirit from a witch for guidance, and it led to disastrous consequences. Let's look again at this passage:

> So Saul died for his transgression which he
> committed against the Lord, even against the

word of the Lord, which he kept not, and also for asking counsel of one that had a familiar spirit, to enquire of it; And enquired not of the Lord: therefore he slew him, and turned the kingdom unto David the son of Jesse (1 Chronicles 10:13-14).

King Saul died for inquiring of the Witch of Endor who had a familiar spirit. This incident is what brought about Saul's death.

One might say, *"God will redeem it. Talking to a witch doesn't make any difference."* God thought it mattered. We are under the misconception that we live in a no-fault world with no-fault divorce, no-fault accidents, and no-fault insurance. It's no one's fault; it's just the way it is. However, the truth of God's Word reveals there are reasons things are the way they are:

"And enquired not of the Lord: therefore he slew him, and turned the kingdom unto David the son of Jesse"
(1 Chronicles 10:14).

Saul, King of Israel, lost his life and kingdom because he listened to the wrong voice. It certainly matters to whom you listen because there are always people who want to talk. Whether it's face-to-face or just to yourself, sometimes you simply need to say, *"I don't want to hear that."* When people try to pull you out of the will of God, off God's plan, and out of God's destiny, it is up to you to say, *"I don't receive that."*

Saul lost his life and his kingdom by leaning on his own devices, by seeking counsel from the wrong sources, by defying the known will of God, and by trusting in the flesh. That is what a wrong voice will do for you.

These are things that can bump you off course and steal your destiny. There is a place God has for you, and sometimes those voices will take you away from that place. Sometimes those voices will take you out of God's timing. That is why you must have good counsel in your life and listen to the right voices.

12

ALWAYS SEEK GOD

In Numbers, chapter 20, we find the children of Israel in the middle of the desert desperate for water. Since Moses is their leader, he has the responsibility of doing something about that. God gave him the instruction, *"Take your rod and hit the rock with it, and water will come out."* Moses obeyed, and the water flowed, resulting in all being satisfied, both people and animals.

Afterward, thirst set in again, and the people complained against Moses. In his anger, what does Moses do? Scripture says he hit the rock again. Wrong move. Why? The rock is a type of Jesus Christ, and Scripture tells us that Jesus will be smitten once for our sin—not twice. The sacrifice that Jesus made is more than enough; there is no need for supplementary sacrifices of any type or number.

It was against God's directive for Moses to hit the rock twice. Therefore, it is blasphemous to believe that there is another sacrifice for sin. Jesus was the sacrifice for our sin, once and for all. Some religious people may say, *"Well, brother, I'm just suffering for my sin, hallelujah!"* They might be suffering the **consequences** of their sin, but they are not qualified to suffer for their sins. No one is holy and righteous enough to do that. The only one who can change your wicked ways is the one who died on Calvary; it was **His blood that was shed.**

Some bad theology came in with the popular Intercessory Prayer Movement several years ago. People claimed they interceded for a person's healing by suffering that same sickness in their own body. In other words, they would take on the person's infirmity and had to pray it out for the person to be healed. When interceding, you may feel the pain or affliction of others in need because empathy helps bear the burdens of the weak. However, you are not qualified to carry what only Jesus can carry. That kind of error will cause the blessing of God to leave a local body. Churches must be careful to guard against error, or there are significant consequences.

Moses received a word from the Lord to hit the rock once. However, he got ahead of God, and without a word from the Lord, he hit the rock a second time in his anger. Doing that cost him dearly, and he was not allowed to enter the Promised Land because of his actions. The consequence of listening to the voice of the flesh—frustration, anger, griping, and complaining—got him out of the will of God—standing on the outside looking in. That can happen to us, too.

FAILURE TO ASK GOD

We can also look at the children of Israel. Do you remember when they went down into the Promised Land, and God gave them a great victory over Jericho? God told them to take the spoils of that victory and bring it all to Him. However, a man named Achan took a portion of those spoils and hid them under the floor of his tent. Let's look at this story in greater detail.

God gave the children of Israel a great victory against the fortified city of Jericho. Next on their radar was this little city called Ai. Without inquiring of the Lord this time, they sent part of their group to battle because it was such a small city. They got ahead of God and were soundly defeated. Several died because they did not first seek the Lord.

Know this: **Just because God blessed one thing at one time does not mean He is going to bless it repeatedly.** When you start moving without inquiring of the Lord, false voices will settle in, and unexpected consequences will occur. You must listen to God every single time.

> ## When you start moving without inquiring of the Lord, false voices will settle in, and unexpected consequences will occur.

Israel asked the Lord how they were defeated by such a small city. He said, *"There is one walking in rebellion to Me and My instruction, and he has hidden My possessions under the floor of their tent."* God allowed them to keep spoils from the battles, but the first-fruit spoils belonged to Him. If they had sought the Lord prior to the battle, the sin in the camp would have been revealed. Here is the account of Achan's confession:

> Achan replied, "I have sinned against the Lord, the God of Israel. For I saw a beautiful robe imported from Babylon, and some silver worth $200, and a bar of gold worth $500. I wanted them so much that I took them, and they are hidden in the ground beneath my tent, with the silver buried deeper than the rest." So Joshua sent some men to search for the loot.

> They ran to the tent and found the stolen
> goods hidden there just as Achan had said,
> with the silver buried beneath the rest. They
> brought it all to Joshua and laid it on the
> ground in front of him. Then Joshua and all
> the Israelites took Achan, the silver, the robe,
> the wedge of gold, his sons, his daughters, his
> oxen, donkeys, sheep, his tent, and everything
> he had, and brought them to the valley of
> Achor. Then Joshua said to Achan, "Why have
> you brought calamity upon us? The Lord will
> now bring calamity upon you." And the men
> of Israel stoned them to death and burned their
> bodies (Joshua 7:20-25, TLB).

Just because we heard from God last year does not mean that old word is still current. God wants to guide you as you walk with Him. Psalm 37:23 says, "The steps of a good man are ordered by the Lord." That means we need step-by-step guidance from our Father God.

How to Get to Your Destiny

You have a destiny; you are headed somewhere. God promises you a vision and a future for your life, but how do you get there? Step by step, one foot in front of the other. Sometimes a step is translated: **STOP or WAIT**, and sometimes the next step is to **TAKE A SIDESTEP**. God's ultimate intention is upward and forward, but sometimes there are lateral steps along the way. Sometimes you must make a move laterally to progress. It is a way to reposition you, to put you in a better spot. God, truly, has our best interests at heart.

MANY VOICES

You can't follow just any voice—whether it's the voice of the disgruntled, a friend, or a close family member. The voice of the Lord is what we follow. Jesus said, "My sheep hear my voice, and I know them, and they follow me" (John 10:27). A similar truth is found in John 10:4, which says: "And when he putteth forth his own sheep, he goeth before them, and the sheep follow him: for they know his voice." There are false voices that will try to steal your destiny. God's sheep hear His voice, and they don't follow any other voice.

We could ask King Saul about other voices who try to steal your destiny. He lost everything because of listening to a witch.

Your destiny is hidden in God, but you must cooperate with it before it can happen. To listen to a voice that takes you away from your purpose will steal your destiny. Just because it is destined does not mean it is inevitable.

"There are, it may be, so many kinds of voices
in the world, and none of them is without signification"
(1 Corinthians 14:10).

There are voices that have significance—a significant place. However, if these voices supersede the voice of the Lord, they are out of place and out of order. Some voices that speak into my life provide counsel I desire to hear. There are places I go to receive guidance. But once the voice of the Lord is known, all discussion is over. Seeking the Lord is one thing, but when you have found Him, your search should cease. The Apostle Paul said this:

> But when it pleased God, who separated me
> from my mother's womb, and called me by his
> grace, To reveal his Son in me, that I might
> preach him among the heathen; immediately I
> conferred not with flesh and blood: (Galatians
> 1:15-16).

Paul was moving out in God's plan to take the gospel to the gentiles. That is his destiny—to preach Christ to the heathen. Then, Paul said, "Immediately I conferred not with flesh and blood." Why? Once he knew the will of God, he knew if he listened to too many voices, they would talk him out of what God called him to do. There would be all kinds of rationalizations and reasonings. There would be all kinds of fear-mongers. There would be everything under the sun that would try to take him out of the plan, will, and purpose of God for his life.

When you hear from God concerning a specific issue, the time to confer with flesh and blood about that same matter —Uncle Morty, Cousin Mavis, your friends at the office, or your golfing buddies—should be considered over.

The word "confer" means to consult together; compare opinions; carry on a discussion or deliberation; to have a conference.

Early in my ministry, I had "experts" trying to talk me out of starting a church. I had everyone under the sun tell me, *"Don't do it!"* After God spoke, I put the blinders on and the earplugs in. It was that literal. I am not going to do anything but what my God tells me to do. Nothing. It was that simple. I must have pleased God in the process because we are still here today.

It is wrong to get counsel **after** you know the will of God, even though we know obtaining godly counsel is also a scriptural principle. When you pursue God's will for your life, godly counsel is essential; however, once you know His will, the talk is over; you must comply with what you heard. If not, there are consequences. Once you know God's will, do it.

Too many voices can talk you out of your destiny. Too many voices can change the word God gave you to a sentence. One of the big processes of following the will of God is elimination. You may have a direction from God, but everyone else wants to add their ideas to it. After a while of doing all the extra things people have added, you may discover you can't even find the will of God anymore. You get tired because you are doing more than you are supposed to be doing. At times like this, we must remember that the Bible says His yoke is easy, and His burden is light.

ENJOY YOUR LIFE!

Do the will of God and enjoy life. One translation says Jesus came to give you life, give it to you to the full, give it to you until you enjoy it. God wants you to enjoy your life. If you are not enjoying life, you are probably not doing the will of God, or you are going about it in the wrong way. Jesus said that He came to give you life and give it to you abundantly. The Gospel of John says:

> The thief cometh not, but for to steal, and to
> kill, and to destroy: I am come that they might
> have life, and that they might have it more
> abundantly (John 10:10).

137

Some may find they are often burdened and stressed. If you are one of those, you are not doing life right. It takes faith to have a Merry Christmas; anyone can have a sad one. It takes faith to enjoy life.

To operate in your destiny means cooperating with the Lord and His plan and keeping the false voices out. Continue to seek Him and do His will, and you will enjoy life.

13

TRUSTING GOD AS YOUR SOURCE

Being able to trust God as your source is vitally important. How can you possibly trust Him with your future if you can't trust Him with your provision? To say you trust God with your future while saying you don't trust Him to be your provider is an absolute conflict. You can't trust God to take you where He wants you to go in your life if you do not trust Him to provide for you along the way.

When I speak of provision, I am not just talking about economics alone; I am referring to everything you need to fulfill your destiny and get to that destination. God has to be the One who arranges things that you cannot arrange and set things in your path that you cannot control—like bringing necessary people into your life. There are some things entirely out of your power that will make a definitive difference in your situation; you must trust God to put those things together in a precise way. That is all a part of the provision of the Lord. If God is your source—which He is—He is your provider as well.

We will continue to look at Abraham's story to draw applicable truth from it. Events from Genesis, chapter 14 were deliberately left out of our discussion up to this point, but we will go back now and pick it up.

In review, here is some background: Lot is Abraham's nephew, and they have already separated from one another. Lot lived in Sodom and Gomorrah before the two areas were famously judged. The king of Sodom was under siege by four predatory kings. In that day, the word "predatory" carried the idea that the strongest king took the possessions of the weaker king. If forces were strong enough, they came and took the other's land, belongings, and possibly the powerless king himself. Let's read the story:

> And they took all the goods of Sodom and Gomorrah, and all their victuals, and went their way. And they took Lot, Abram's brother's son, who dwelt in Sodom, and his goods, and departed. And there came one that had escaped, and told Abram the Hebrew; for he dwelt in the plain of Mamre the Amorite, brother of Eshcol, and brother of Aner: and these were confederate with Abram (Genesis 14:11-13).

These kings came in and took the possessions of Sodom and Gomorrah, along with Lot and his goods. Interestingly, Abram was called "the Hebrew" here, and the Hebrew people had not yet come into existence. This reference was a foreshadowing of what would be the Hebrew people.

Think about this: Abram has only 318 men somewhat trained in warfare who are going to do battle with four kings and their armies. It was a pretty brave endeavor.

> And when Abram heard that his brother was taken captive, he armed his trained servants, born in his own house, three hundred and

eighteen, and pursued them unto Dan. And he
divided himself against them, he and his
servants, by night, and smote them, and
pursued them unto Hobah, which is on the left
hand of Damascus. And he brought back all the
goods, and also brought again his brother Lot,
and his goods, and the women also, and the
people (Genesis 14:14-16).

Abram and his relatively small army delivered the people and
goods that were captured. He won the victory and brought the
people back.

And the **king of Sodom** went out to meet
[Abram] after his return from the slaughter of
Chedorlaomer, and of the kings that were with
him, at the valley of Shaveh, which is the king's
dale. And Melchizedek **king of Salem** brought
forth bread and wine: and he was the priest of
the most high God. And he blessed him, and
said, Blessed by Abram of the most high God,
possessor of heaven and earth: And blessed be
the most high God, which hath delivered thine
enemies into thy hand. And he gave him tithes
of all. And the **king of Sodom** said unto
Abram, Give me the persons, and take the
goods to thyself (Genesis 14:17-21, emphasis
added).

That is precisely what the devil says today, *"You take the stuff
and give me the people. I just want the souls."* This is how he
works.

ABRAM'S TITHE

Through battle, Abram acquired the possessions of the four kings. When he returned with the spoils of war, he gave tithes to Melchizedek. This Scripture tells us that Melchizedek is called the king of Salem, otherwise known as Jerusalem. This high priest was also king of Jerusalem. In typology, Melchizedek is a type of Christ as explained in Hebrews 7:

> For this Melchizedek, king of Salem, priest of the most high God, who met Abraham returning from the slaughter of the kings, and blessed him; To whom also Abraham gave a tenth part of all; first being by interpretation King of righteousness, and after that also King of Salem, which is, King of peace; Without father, without mother, without descent, having neither beginning of days, nor end of life; but made like unto the Son of God; abideth a priest continually. Now consider how great this man was, unto whom even the patriarch Abraham gave the tenth of the spoils (Hebrews 7:1-4).

Scripture references Melchizedek as a type of the Son of God or a type of Jesus Christ. He is called the King of Righteousness and the King of Salem, which means peace. Abram brings tithes to this priest who represents the Christ. In the New Testament, we bring tithes to the King of Kings and the Lord of Lords; we do not pay tithes to the church. What do I mean by that? Is the church the place where you tithe? Of course, it is, but it is only because the church represents Jesus Christ. We do not tithe to the church just to support the institution; tithing is an act of worship to Christ, our Redeemer, who is our Savior.

Let's read on in this story:

> And the king of Sodom said unto Abram, Give
> me the persons, and take the goods to thyself.
> And Abram said to the king of Sodom, I have
> lift up mine hand unto the Lord, the most high
> God, the possessor of heaven and earth. That
> I will not take from a thread even to a
> shoelatchet, and that I will not take any thing
> that is thine, lest thou shouldest say, I have
> made Abram rich: (Genesis 14:21-23).

Abram was making a declaration, probably as much to himself
as to those around him. The Bible says Abraham believed God,
and it was counted as righteousness (Genesis 15:6). This was an
act of Abram's faith in operation when he boldly declared,
*"King, I don't want a misunderstanding between you and me in
any way. You are not my source. My God alone is my source."*

To flow in your destiny or to reach your God-appointed
destination, I believe there comes a point in your life where you
are going to have to say those exact words. The characters and
circumstances are different, but the internal act is the same.
We come to a place inside ourselves where we make that same
declaration: God is my source. If you do not, you will spend
your life living by the devices of the flesh or human reasoning,
or whatever or whomever you can maneuver around.

If you live by the flesh, you will become a manipulator,
conniver, or schemer. You will believe that you have the power
to meet your needs by your own devices and abilities. How
short-sighted it would be for us to believe that we even

understand our needs. We have no idea what we will need, let alone how we will provide for it.

There is a place we all reach. It could be a crisis moment, or it may be a challenge from God's Word. I do not know where or what it is, but I can tell you there is a time coming in your life when you will have to make the declaration that you actually believe that God alone can be your source of supply. If you don't do that, then you will be bound to live by the system of this world. You will have to rely on your own devices—how you can figure it out to get circumstances to line up—because you have no divine supply until you make that choice.

MY STORY

Nora and I came to that place a long time ago. I remember when God called us to step into our destiny. We stepped out in faith with no assets, no money, nothing in the literal sense. When we started our church, we had no denomination to underwrite us. There was no building where we could meet and no congregation to listen to us. We had nothing.

We went full-time into the ministry from day one, thinking either God is our source or we are fools. We threw ourselves on Him and said, *"Lord, we don't have any power to do this. It's either sink or swim based on Your provision."* It has been that way ever since. In the beginning, it was nip and tuck. However, everything we sacrificed to follow God and more has been added back in the long run. It does cost you something to make the sacrifice, but God has been more than enough for us.

We have tithed for years. Both Nora and I grew up in tithing families; that was a part of our upbringing. However, I had no idea back then that when I tithed, I could trust God to be my source. I did not know these Scriptures; I just recognized the tithe as a religious exercise, so I tithed but put no faith in the process. I knew it was the right thing to do, but I did not realize that I was actively entering into a covenant with God to be my provider. I was far into my adult years before I understood that tithing was much more serious than I had thought.

When you do things beyond your knowledge, God will still bless you. It does help, however, to have faith in your actions. I did not know you could believe God for things while being obedient; people reason that it is selfish and presumptuous. How is it presumption when I do my part, and He does His? It's not presumption to believe God; it is obedience and faith in Him. He is never offended by it. However, He will get offended by people limiting Him.

The children of Israel limited Him, and the Bible says He was not well-pleased with that. If you limit God, He is displeased, but He is not upset by someone trusting Him. He wants to be your provider.

THE TITHE

We discussed earlier that an altar is a place where business takes place—a place of exchange. The deal or covenant is between you and God. I am not talking about financial deals; I am talking about spiritual arrangements. We build an altar because we believe something. Our God, the Most-High, will not let us down. After all, He is the Possessor of heaven and earth.

Abram's response to the king of Sodom was something like this:

COOPERATING WITH YOUR DESTINY

I do not even want a shoelace. I don't want anything that is yours in the event that you would say you made me rich. Just return our food provisions. We don't want anything else you have because we don't need it.

To acquiesce to the king's "generosity" would put Abram in a differential or submissive role to him, and everyone would have known it. That's when Abram made his declaration, *"God is my source."*

We know that a tithe is a tenth. Abram gave a tenth of the spoils to the king of Salem; however, this is not just about money. Tithing is about trusting God to be the source for everything in your life because you need so many things beyond money, like healing, for example. Money will not get you that. How about restoring your marriage? Money will not get you that, either. What about your son or daughter who has totally gone off the rails and needs to come back to the Lord? Money certainly will not get you that. What if your career goes belly-up? Tithing honors the God of your destiny! When you have a major change and don't have a way to step over into your destiny under your own power, He is still the God of your destiny. He is the One who makes a way—the One who provides, the One who sets it all in motion. He is your provider.

If you do not come to terms with the fact that God is your source, you will needlessly struggle through life in ways you cannot yet imagine. You will have fears for which the world has no solutions. Some wring their hands and worry; however, you must trust God. The same God that brought me to this point is the same God that will take me to the next. The same God that brought you into this world is the same God that will

146

take you to your destination at the end. All you have to do is trust Him. Here's what the Bible says about trust:

"I've been young and I've been old and I've never seen the righteous forsaken, nor His seed out begging bread" (Psalm 37:5).

God is your provider. God is your Source. He is who we look to for everything. When the world says you should give up—cash it in—just say no! A hundred times NO! Within you is the One who is greater than this world.

What are you going to do if the economy collapses? Eat! What are you going to do if there is a catastrophic electromagnetic pulse from a nuclear weapon? Eat!

God can save by many or by few; His hand is not short, nor His power slack concerning you. Your destiny is in Him, not in your abilities, nor the abilities of those around you. At the end of the day, you are required to trust Him alone. That is what this book is about.

When Abraham brought his tithe to Melchizedek, it was a stake pounded in the ground; it was an altar built. It was also a declaration of his trust in God.

He left the city of Ur and his family, and Abraham began to march to a place, but he knew not where. He had to trust God every step of the way, but the Bible says he became one of the richest men in the land by doing it. In the end, what he sacrificed to follow God didn't cost him anything. He died full of provision at an old age because he declared His trust in God as his source.

A tithe declares your provision has come from God; it is directed toward God. You are bringing your tithe as a form of worship unto the Lord, declaring that your provision has come from Him. A tithe expresses your trust in God's power to supply all your needs, and it separates you from the world; you are different. A tithe is a token or sign of a covenant and honors the Lord. The blessing of the ten percent tithe comes on the other ninety percent and sanctifies or sets it apart. A tithe is an expression of your faith and separates you from the devil and the world's system. Tithing was Abram's way of saying that he was all in for the Lord. Where your treasure is, there is your heart. So, until you come to that place, you are not all in; you are only in part of the way.

Money Answers All Things

How can we ever fulfill our destiny if we cannot trust God to be our provider? It is not even possible; it is a total contradiction in terms. You cannot trust Him with your future if you cannot trust Him with your present supply. Isn't that what your future is about?

If God told you to go to China tomorrow, what would your answer be? Think before you answer. Do you have the money? You may be willing, but willing doesn't pay the bills! The Bible says that money answers all things:

> "Feasting makes you happy and wine cheers you
> up, but you can't have either without money"
> (Ecclesiastes 10:19, GNT).

Every time I take a mission trip, I have to pay for it—no freebies anywhere. Think about your situation. If God told you

He wanted you to go around the world to preach His Gospel, could you do it? Not on $11.00 and some pocket change you couldn't! Money makes the world "go-round" and allows you to go around it. If going around the world is your destiny, money will come into play; you cannot bypass that. When **God** tells you to do something, His provision is understood.

How are you going to have provision when you rob God? The Bible says we rob God in our tithes and offerings:

> "Will a man rob God? Yet ye have robbed me. But ye say, Wherein have we robbed thee? In tithes and offerings." (Malachi 3:8).

If you are stealing from God, you have not entered into that covenant of provision. If God is your source, your destiny includes your provision. Either God is your Provider, or you are looking to your own devices or the world. It is not possible to have it both ways.

IS TITHING UNDER THE LAW?

Some people say that tithing is Old Testament and is under the law and conclude that we do not tithe in the New Testament. There's one problem with that logic: Hebrews chapter seven is in the New Testament, which retells the story of Abraham and Melchizedek. If tithing was under the law and this story occurred before the law, tithing cannot be under the law. Tithing took place before the law was written. So tithing is not under the law. Tithing is a relationship and covenant that we share and enjoy with God.

The Bible tells us:

> According as his divine power hath given unto
> us all things that pertain unto life and godliness,
> through the knowledge of him that hath called
> us to glory and virtue (2 Peter 1:3).

God has given you everything you need to fulfill your destiny—
"all things that pertain unto life and godliness." According to
Scripture, everything that you need to live a godly life is
provided. You may not be experiencing this in your life because
you have not walked in the covenant. You have not yet allowed
God to be your provider. You may be looking to the world's
devices rather than trusting Him. The only way you can show
trust is by your actions; trust is not a feeling. It might affect
your feelings, but trust is an action. You are required to act on
it. The Bible says:

> **After these things** the word of the Lord came
> unto Abram in a vision, saying, Fear not,
> Abram: I am thy shield, and thy exceeding great
> reward (Genesis 15:1, emphasis added).

This verse indicates that after the events involving the tithe to
Melchizedek, God made this proclamation to Abram. It is
saying, *"After the tithe took place, I'll be your protector and your
provider."* Let's read on down through the chapter:

> And Abram said, Lord God, what wilt thou
> give me, seeing I go childless, and the steward
> of my house is this Eliezer of Damascus? And
> Abram said, Behold, to me thou hast given no
> seed: and, lo, one born in my house is mine heir.

And behold, the word of the Lord came unto him, saying, This shall not be thine heir; but he that shall come forth out of thine own bowels shall be thine heir. And he brought him forth abroad, and said, Look now toward heaven, and tell the stars, if thou be able to number them: and he said unto him, So shall thy seed be. And he believed in the Lord; and he counted it to him for righteousness. And he said unto him, I am the Lord that brought thee out of Ur of the Chaldees, to give thee this land to inherit it. And he said, Lord God, whereby shall I know that I shall inherit it? (Genesis 15:2-8).

In other words, Abram is dealing with this internally by saying, *"Okay Lord, I hear You, but I'm struggling some over this because it's new to me. I haven't been here before. I don't have the book of Genesis to turn to and read."* So, right out of the box, he said, *"Lord, what is in it for me? What will you give me?"*

TITHING ALLOWS YOU TO BRING AN OFFERING

Abraham is the father of our faith (Romans 4:16). We are following his example, but he did not have a pattern to emulate. As we saw earlier, Abraham wanted to know what was in it for him. Following that up, he said, *"How am I going to know it? Confirm it to me, Lord. This is critical to me. I am giving my life to this thing. Firm it up in me. I am willing to do it."* Both you and I have asked the same questions.

That is a fair question. It's your life, after all. Listen to how God responded:

> And he said unto him, "Take me an heifer of
> three years old, and a she goat of three years old,
> and a ram of three years old, and a turtledove,
> and a young pigeon. And he took unto him all
> these, and divided them in the midst, and laid
> each piece one against another: but the birds
> divided he not" (Genesis 15:9-10).

Abraham's destiny began to be fulfilled when he acknowledged God as his Source through his tithing. God could have answered him through any means He wanted—a burning bush, pillar of light, or someone walking on water. He could have done anything, but what did God say? *"Bring Me an offering if you want confirmation."* Abraham's response was one step further into his destiny.

When you tithe, God opens the windows of heaven (Malachi 3:10), but when you bring Him an offering, He pours what you need through those open windows and into your life. Tithing gets the windows open. Offerings bring His blessings through them.

God does not always request an offering. In this case, He asked for one. Giving an offering is something we do intentionally; that is what makes it an offering. The Bible says the tithe is holy and belongs to the Lord. A tithe is not an offering; it is an acknowledgment that you and God are in relationship.

> And all the **tithe** of the land, whether of the
> seed of the land, or of the fruit of the tree, is the
> Lord's: it is holy unto the Lord (Leviticus 27:30,
> emphasis added).

When we bring God that which is already His, it's not an offering. It is only an offering when we bring God what is ours. The tithe is already His, and we bring an offering of our own free will. Abram asked God to confirm his destiny, and in this case, God asked Abram for an offering. God told him to build an altar, and they would have an exchange. Scripture tells us not to go to God empty-handed (Deuteronomy 16:16) because a man's gift will make room for him, and that is not referring to your gifting or talent (Proverbs 18:16). A tithe is not a gift; a tithe is what makes the gift acceptable. Bringing a gift or offering to God without first giving Him the tithe is unacceptable.

Abram brought his offering to the Lord:

> And it came to pass, that, when the sun went down, and it was dark, behold a smoking furnace, and a burning lamp that passed between those pieces (Genesis 15:17).

This verse describes the glory of God coming on Abram's offering—the fire of God coming into this man's existence. God's glory shining bright indicates He is bringing your destiny to pass by coming into your life in a significant way. God received the offering because Abram is a tither. The tithe opens the door for God to receive the offering. When he brings the offering to the Lord, the glory of God comes into his life. Notice this verse:

> **In the same day** the Lord made a covenant with Abram, saying, Unto thy seed have I given this land, from the river of Egypt unto the great river, the river Euphrates: (Genesis 15:18, emphasis added).

This verse speaks of an everlasting covenant between Abraham and God, and his seed will have all that God promised. Regardless of what anyone says or tries to take from them, God continues to watch over that covenant with no one able to alter or change it.

To understand God, you must understand covenant. The New Covenant summarized is: Jesus hung on Cavalry, He shed His blood, and He gave His life to make a covenant with you. And the Bible says God could swear by no one greater, so He swore by Himself (Hebrews 6:13). In other words, He is saying:

> *I'm not calling in the cavalry to enforce this covenant because anyone I could call to implement it is not as big as Me. I, God Almighty, will make a covenant with you, and I will take your case and cut covenant with you. I promise you that I will see to it that everything in My plan and purpose that you have said "yes" to comes to pass without any flaws, delays, subversions, intrusions, or anything else that the enemy would bring to stop it. I promise you that I will bring this thing to pass because you are a tither and a giver—you obey Me in your giving. I will covenant with you for your destiny.*

You have a destiny in God, but if God is not your provider, you will never get there. Either He is your supply, or He is not. If the Lord is not your supply, you are on your own, and your destiny will not materialize. I am talking to you about cooperating with your destiny; either God is your source, or He is not.

154

THE TITHE IS HOLY

The tithe is the Lord's, and it is holy. It does not belong to us; it belongs to Him. When we withhold the tithe, we are taking our destiny back into our own hands. When we choose not to tithe, we do not trust. We are establishing our own lot; we rely on our own power; we trust in ourselves more than we believe in God. Here is this verse in another translation:

> "Ten percent of everything you harvest is holy
> and it belongs to Me, whether it grows in your fields
> or on your fruit trees" (Leviticus 27:30, CEV).

Ten percent of everything you have already belongs to God. You cannot "give" the Lord a tithe; it is a contradiction of terms. You may **give it back** to Him, but the tithe is already His. You cannot give Him what already belongs to Him.

Let's look at an illustration of this. I don't like a bunch of heavy things in my pocket when I minister, so I keep my car keys in my study when I preach. If someone brought my keys to me would they be giving me, the right to drive my car? No, because I already had that right. They just gave me something that already belonged to me. In much the same way, when we bring the tithe to the Lord, we are not actually giving it to the Lord; rather, we are **giving it back** to the Lord out of what He has given to us. The tithe serves as a test to see if we will obey Him.

God tests us with the tithe. The command to tithe comes as a test to see if we will obey Him with money. Your **offering** is what you do out of your own goodwill. Sometimes the Lord will tell you to give an offering, saying something like, *"Hey Ed, if you'll notice, there are some people over there struggling. I want* *you to pay their light bill for them.*" That would be an offering. The Bible says that he who gives to the poor lends to the Lord, and the Lord will repay it, and He will (Proverbs 19:17).

Jesus said, "But seek ye first the kingdom of God, and his righteousness; and all these things shall be added unto you" (Matthew 6:33). Through the tithe, Abraham put God first. He obeyed God with the offering and entered into a covenant with Him for his destiny.

Do you see health and healing in Abraham's covenant anywhere? You do not just need money to fulfill your destiny; you require a body that is worthy of the walk. There are a lot of things contained in this covenant. This is not a money message; it is a destiny covenant message between you and God. You have covenanted with God about your purpose in life. That is huge!

When you put God first—in control of your life and destiny, everything you need for life will be added unto you. He becomes your provider, and things happen. Remember, we are to follow the faith of Abraham because the Bible is written for our instruction, edification, and knowledge. If it worked for Abraham, it will work for us. The Bible was not given for us to read a bunch of stories; God gave us the Bible to instruct us on how to live this life successfully.

14

PARTNERING IN GOD'S WORK

> For there is no difference between the Jew and
> the Greek: for the same Lord over all is rich
> unto all that **call** upon him. For whosoever
> shall **call** upon the name of the Lord shall be
> saved. How then shall they **call** on him in
> whom they have not believed? and how shall
> they believe in him of whom they have not
> heard? and how shall they hear without a
> preacher? (Romans 10:12-14, emphasis
> added).

As we examine these verses, the first keyword to focus on is the
word "call" in verse 13. We use this passage when we talk to
people about the Lord, making sure they understand that
everyone who **calls** on the Lord will be saved.

The Message Bible translates verse 14 as saying, "But how can
people call for help if they don't know who to trust? And how
can they know who to trust if they haven't heard of the One
who can be trusted?" (Romans 10:14, MSG).

This verse tells us that it is impossible to call if you have no
belief base. Before you can call, you must believe. You cannot

call unless you believe, and you cannot believe unless you've heard. You must hear; someone must tell you.

SPREADING THE GOOD NEWS

My wife, Nora, and I have a mutual friend with a business that we frequent. One day I realized I didn't know if she was a Christian, so I started praying for her. We need to start thinking and praying about others because people can't call on the Lord before believing, and they can't believe unless they first hear. Someone must say something. Because of this friend's background, she may live in a world where she has never heard about the Savior, Jesus; she may never hear about Him if we don't speak up. God may have brought us into her life for this reason. We need to be respectful of others, but neither are we ashamed to share our faith.

You can start a conversation by simply asking, *"Do you know God has a wonderful plan for your life? There is some wonderful news that I would like to share with you. Have you heard about this man Jesus?"* There is no religious place to hide now. However, if you tell people up front that you're a Christian, people have to work through their religious thinking before they can hear you.

Read this powerful passage again:

> How then shall they call on him in whom they
> have not believed? and how shall they believe in
> him of whom they have not heard? and how
> shall they hear without a preacher? And how
> shall they preach, except they be sent? as it is
> written, How beautiful are the feet of them that

preach the gospel of peace, and bring glad
tidings of good things! (Romans 10:14-15).

We have some key phrases here:

1) People can't call until they first believe.
2) They can't believe unless they hear.
3) They can't hear without a preacher.
4) Preachers can't preach unless they're sent.

The "beautiful feet" reference is an interesting point. It's not
said because someone has two great-looking feet replete with
ten gorgeous toes. Feet are beautiful because of the message
that they carry. When you were lost and undone, without God
and His Son, someone came and told you about Jesus. To you,
the person who brought you that message will have beautiful
feet throughout eternity. This passage goes on to say:

> But they have not all obeyed the gospel. For
> Esaias saith, Lord, who hath believed our
> report? So then faith cometh by hearing, and
> hearing by the word of God. But I say, Have
> they not heard? Yes verily, their sound went
> into all the earth, and their words unto the
> ends of the world (Romans 10:16-18).

This entire passage is not just dealing with the routines of life.
The Bible says here that their words of salvation went to the
ends of the world. God tells us to send this gospel to the ends
of the earth in one form or another.

I came to understand a long time ago that I can't physically go
to the ends of the world by myself. It is not possible. Even Jesus

COOPERATING WITH YOUR DESTINY

knew His limitations. He said it was better and more expedient to go away to heaven because if He didn't, the Comforter would not come to help us (John 16:7). Jesus knew He couldn't touch as many people as He wanted to because of the physical limitations of being only one person on this planet. So, He sent the Holy Spirit to come and live in His people so that the body of Christ could absolutely saturate this earth with the gospel. To cover the earth, we each have an ever-growing specific sphere of influence—a particular arena or world that we live in—where we minister to others.

Vicariously, through the activities of others, we can touch parts of the world that otherwise, we could never assist. We can go places that we could never go to under normal circumstances. I may not be able to go everywhere, but we can support missionaries that do. We can't partner with every minister or good cause, but we support those as the Lord leads us.

PARTNERSHIPS IN THE KINGDOM

We are thankful for those we can support, but we also know there is more to do. Instead of excusing our inabilities to reach everyone, we reach those we can. Instead of cursing the darkness, light a candle. Light the world around us, and then use our power and ability through partnering with others to enable them to do what they can do. What we cannot do, others can.

"Do something lest you do nothing."

Let's look at an interesting letter in the book of Philippians:

> Paul and Timotheus, the servants of Jesus
> Christ, to all the saints in Christ Jesus which
> are at Philippi, with the bishops and deacons:
> Grace be unto you, and peace, from God our
> Father, and from the Lord Jesus Christ. I
> thank my God upon every remembrance of
> you, Always in every prayer of mine for you all
> making request with joy, For your fellowship
> in the gospel from the first day until now
> (Philippians 1:1-5).

In this passage of Scripture, Paul used the word "fellowship." Sometimes we fail to look with the depth God desires, and we miss its real meaning. The term "fellowship" is a word that some Bible translations have translated *partnership*.

This letter was written by Paul to his partners—those who supported the gospel. It's an example of what we read in Romans about those who couldn't go, but they made the trip possible for Paul. Those people became partners with him in spreading the gospel.

I'm sure you noticed that Paul used affectionate phrases while addressing his partners; he said, "I thank God for you," and "I thank my God upon every remembrance of you." He was addressing all those who partnered with him in his activities. He reassured them that they held a special place in his heart. Paul goes on to say:

> For your fellowship in the gospel from the first
> day until now; Being confident of this very
> thing, that he which hath begun a good work

in you will perform it until the day of Jesus
Christ: (Philippians 1:5-6).

Paul, speaking by unction and inspiration of the Holy Spirit,
expressed that when God started something in and through his
partners, He would complete it. Paul understood that it is not
enough simply to begin something; we must finish with God's
help.

Paul is undoubtedly saying, *"I'm sure that what you've started
will be completed."* I'm certain that promise covered a myriad of
different activities in their lives; their partnership with him
would be one part. It could also be the work God was doing
through them—the thing to which He called each one. Paul
said he was confident that what God started in them would not
be cut short before it is finished. Remember, he was not writing
this letter to everyone, only his partners.

Look at the next verse:

> Even as it is meet for me to think this of you all,
> because I have you in my heart; inasmuch as
> both in my bonds, and in the defence and
> confirmation of the gospel, ye all are partakers
> of my grace (Philippians 1:7).

Paul told his partners, "I have you in my heart."

We know from Scripture that Paul was in prison for this gospel
on many occasions. He was also stoned with rocks for the
gospel. We have no record of his partners ever being stoned or
imprisoned for the gospel. The essence of what he said was,
"In my time of distress and difficulty, you stood with me. You were

my partners in this gospel that I preach. You are partakers of my grace."

"Grace" is a word that we often use especially relating to salvation. Saving grace comes to us when we make Jesus Christ the Lord of our lives. The Bible also teaches that there are grace giftings in our lives. It's when God touches you in a unique way that makes it easy for you to do what is difficult for someone else. You have been gifted and graced by God to do certain things you are uniquely designed to do.

A good example would be the musicians and singers in a church service. They are particularly graced in a way that I am not. I can enjoy what God's doing with them, and their gift blesses me, but I couldn't do that even if my feet were on fire. Why? I don't have the grace for it. In my opinion, I sound great in the shower and alone in my car, but that's it.

Paul said that when you partner with a ministry, the grace resting on that ministry comes on you. In other words, there is a favor that comes on you. A way to say this for shock value is that, in a sense, you can buy an anointing. *"What?! The anointing comes from God, and you can't buy an anointing."* It's true that you cannot buy from God what He's unwilling to give; you can't manipulate Him. That is a certainty. But, now that I have your attention, let me say it this way:

There are anointings and graces that you need in your life that, if you invest in a person or ministry who has that particular grace, that same grace can come upon you.

COOPERATING WITH YOUR DESTINY

I'm not saying that if I invest in someone who is gifted to sing, I'm suddenly going to be gifted to sing like them. But I will say that the favor that comes on that singer when they stand in that role can come on me if I invest in it. I hope you understand what I'm saying in context. Paul said, *"As my partners, you are all partakers of my grace."* That is important for you to understand.

VARIOUS COVENANTS

You absolutely should read the book of Philippians sometime front to back in one sitting; read it like a letter that Paul wrote to his partners, and it will then make much more sense to you. You will begin to see things from it that you did not otherwise see. Philippians is part of God's Holy Word; we all glean from it, receive blessings from it, and see the principles of it. In that regard, it is written to us all. However, this was a unique letter written to people who were doing a particular thing related to their covenant with Paul in the ministry. When I use the word "covenant," I'm talking about a solemn, binding agreement between parties. That is what a partner is.

In the same manner, when Nora and I married, we became life partners. The Bible says God witnessed the covenant made at our marriage. That partnership is a covenant.

There are covenants at many levels. The ultimate covenant we walk in is the one we make with God Almighty, which was cut in blood—Jesus' blood was shed to give us that covenant. The word "testament" means *covenant*; when you say "New Testament," you are actually saying *New Covenant*. You may not understand all about it, but the writers certainly did. As we grow in the Lord, we should come into more of an understanding of it.

There are also others with whom we make covenants. For example, if you visit a bank for a mortgage to buy that new home you want, you and the bank enter into a covenant represented by the mortgage. You are now in covenant with that bank, and you agree to certain things while they agree to certain things. If the covenant is honored, everything will work properly. If all the terms and conditions are met and the people are honest, everything will work out fine. You will not have any trouble with the covenant unless someone breaks it. If you do not pay what you are supposed to pay, you break the covenant. If the bank starts charging you five percent more on the loan than agreed upon, they broke the covenant. There are ways we can violate a covenant agreement.

I want you to understand that there are various levels of covenants. Another is our marriage covenant, while another is our covenant agreements in business. In addition, you have a covenant with the government that you will obey the laws; if you run a stop sign, you broke the covenant, and there are consequences. However, our ultimate covenant is with God.

CHURCH COVENANT

I grew up in church, and back in the day, we had an attendance board on the wall near the front. Right above the attendance board, they posted what they called a "church covenant." The church covenant stated that you would be a faithful and loyal member, and if you were to leave that church, you would be diligent to find a church near you and that type of thing. That was a church covenant.

The day you came into the body of Christ, you entered into a church covenant. Some are ignorant of that truth, and some don't care, but it's a real thing to God. Ignorance does not exempt us from the reality of it. When we become a Christian, we enter into a covenant with the body of Christ. It is outlined very clearly in 1 Corinthians 11, where it talks about us partaking of the body of the Lord Jesus Christ—what we call communion—the covenant meal of the bread and the wine or the blood and the bread.

> I have already told you what the Lord Jesus did on the night he was betrayed. And it came from the Lord himself. He took some bread in his hands. Then after he had given thanks, he broke it and said, "This is my body, which is given for you. Eat this and remember me." After the meal, Jesus took a cup of wine in his hands and said, "This is my blood, and with it God makes his new agreement with you. Drink this and remember me." The Lord meant that when you eat this bread and drink from this cup, you tell about his death until he comes (1 Corinthians 11:23-26, CEV).

If we don't recognize the relationship that we share with the body of Christ, the Bible says the result is less than stellar:

> So then, you should each examine yourself first, and then eat the bread and drink from the cup. For if you do not recognize the meaning of the Lord's body when you eat the bread and drink from the cup, you bring judgment on yourself as you eat and drink. That is why many of you are sick and weak, and several have died. If we would examine ourselves first, we would not

come under God's judgment (1 Corinthians 11:28-31, GNT).

In a nutshell, this verse says that many of these people are weak and sick and die before their time because they didn't recognize their covenant with the body of Christ.

As Christians, we enter that covenant, whether we realize it or not. When we take communion, it is a covenant meal. Paul was in a covenant relationship with these Philippian believers as a preacher of the gospel. He told them, "For to me to live is Christ, and to die is gain" (Philippians 1:21). I believe any of us that walk with the Lord could make that statement. We gain when we leave this earth. I don't want to leave before it's time, but when the time comes, there is nothing to hold me here.

PAUL'S DILEMMA

> For to me, living means opportunities for Christ, and dying—well, that's better yet! But if living will give me more opportunities to win people to Christ, then I really don't know which is better, to live or die! Sometimes I want to live, and at other times I don't, for I long to go and be with Christ. How much happier for me than being here! But the fact is that I can be of more help to you by staying! (Philippians 1:21-24, TLB).

The Apostle Paul was saying:

> *There's a challenge for me to live in the flesh and continue the fruit of my labor. I'm having difficulty choosing to stay and keep working for*

the Kingdom or go home to heaven and be
with the Lord face-to-face.

Have you heard that old saying, "I'm between a rock and a hard place"? This is a perfect example of that saying. He had two things going on; he wanted both and was not sure which one would win. He said: "For I am in a strait betwixt two, having a desire to depart, and to be with Christ; which is far better" (Philippians 1:23). Notice that he felt going to heaven was a far better choice for him personally. Paul said, "Nevertheless, to abide in the flesh is more needful for you" (Philippians 1:24).

Do you see Paul's dilemma? If he were living for himself, he would go ahead and take his trip to heaven; however, he was not living for himself only. He said, *"Since you need me, I'll put my desires to the side, and I'll live this thing out for you."* The benefit of his partners was a crucial component in his decision. These people—his partners—were foremost in his thinking and his heart. As Christians, we don't walk at that level of self-sacrifice with just anyone.

I was talking to a military general who is a strong man of faith. His wife had recently gone to heaven, and he was ready to go and be with her. In that conversation, he said something I will never forget: *"The only thing that I'm glad about her dying is that she doesn't have to feel what I feel."* When you care enough about someone else to bear incredible pain and loss to keep them from experiencing it, that is true love.

I know this feeling, but I doubt it is at the level that Paul felt. When you're in ministry, you will have to overcome levels of self-will, as the Apostle Paul described. You'll find that some of your flock—those you minister to—are not partners in the gospel; they are mere listeners. Partners in the gospel are different, and that's who Paul was talking about here. He said they are my partners in the faith, and I am living my life for them.

Do you understand the power of that covenant? Many people don't recognize it, but that does not change how serious it is.

Allow me to share a personal experience with you regarding this covenant principle. My wife and I received a letter from someone in the ministry that we have supported for many years, and they are involved in a big project. If I listened to my flesh, I might say, *"They need several million dollars for that? They don't need that!"* Instead, I told Nora, *"I don't know what they have to deal with, and I don't know what they believe from God, so, send them some money."* From where I sit, they don't need it, but since I don't know what I don't know, send them some money. I have partnered with them for years, and I am certainly not going to stop now. Why would I care about that—just because I think it's unnecessary? I don't know what God has called them to do, and I don't know their mission, but I am a partner, so I'm investing. Case closed.

Paul's decision to remain on the earth was based on his love for his partners, not his love for the gospel, not really even his love for Jesus. Of course, it was the will of Jesus for the partners to grow and mature, so ultimately, it goes back to that. But, if his partners were taken out of the equation, he would have gone on to heaven in a flash.

PARTNERSHIP IS TWO-SIDED

"But the LORD said unto me, Say not, I am a child: for thou shalt go to all that I shall send thee, and whatsoever I command thee thou shalt speak" (Jeremiah 1:7).

COOPERATING WITH YOUR DESTINY

God told Jeremiah to go to all the people where He sent him. You do not partner with everyone, only those to whom God sends you. However, it's not just a one-way street. It's not just Paul living for his partners; it's his partners living, in a sense, for him and his mission. They recognized they were part of the call on his life. There is much that can be said about relationships through partnership.

Another good illustration is found in 2 Kings. This story moves me a great deal every time I read it. Let's look at it:

> And it fell on a day, that Elisha passed to Shunem, where was a great woman; and she constrained him to eat bread. And so it was, that as oft as he passed by, he turned in thither to eat bread (2 Kings 4:8).

Being a great woman meant she was a woman of substance— a wealthy woman. Elisha would travel that road quite a bit, and every time he came through town, he would stop and eat with them. They showed him great hospitality.

> And she said unto her husband, Behold now, I perceive that this is an holy man of God, which passeth by us continually. Let us make a little chamber, I pray thee, on the wall; and let us set for him there a bed, and a table, and a stool, and a candlestick: and it shall be, when he cometh to us, that he shall turn in thither (2 Kings 4:9-10).

When you read these verses, don't have the idea of meager fare. In other words, sometimes people talk about the prophet's chamber as only needing a candle, stool, and bed. This couple was preparing the prophet a place to refresh himself for the work of the ministry.

> And it fell on a day, that he came thither, and he turned into the chamber, and lay there. And he said to Gehazi his servant, Call this Shunammite. And when he had called her, she stood before him. And he said unto him, Say now unto her, Behold, thou hast been careful for us with all this care; what is to be done for thee? (2 Kings 4:11-13a).

In other words, he was saying, *"You have taken diligent care of us. Now, what can I do for you?"* Notice the open-endedness of this request: What do you want? What request can we fulfill? Her care for partnering with a man of God's ministry qualified her for a *"what can I do for you"* question from the man of God.

The Shunammite woman affirmed to Elisha that she was fine and had no earthly needs. As the story goes on, the servant Gehazi has a profound idea. The next verse reports, "And he said, What then is to be done for her? And Gehazi answered, Verily she hath no child, and her husband is old" (2 Kings 4:14).

This woman had all the provision and wealth she needed; she didn't need food, clothing, housing, or favor with the government. However, she did not have a child; her hopelessness caused her not to bring up the subject. For a woman of that time, she never would be considered fruitful if she was childless. Let's see what Elisha did:

And he said, Call her. And when he had called
her, she stood in the door. And he said, About
this season, according to the time of life, thou
shalt embrace a son. And she said, Nay, my
lord, thou man of God, do not lie unto thine
handmaid (2 Kings 4:15-16).

In other words, *"By this time next year. you are going to have a
child—a little boy."* But, she said, *"Don't play with my emotions
about this. This is not a joke to me. If it is not real, drop it."*
Regarding this subject, she had absolute hopelessness; she
didn't want to discuss it. So, what happened?

How many prayers do you think you have to pray to get to the
point where you totally give it up? Is it the place where
frustration is heaped on frustration on top of frustration? That's
where she was.

"And the woman conceived, and bare a son at
that season that Elisha had said unto her, according
to the time of life" (2 Kings 4:17).

God knew her situation and gave her what she was unwilling
to ask for—the deepest and most important thing in her life—
because she partnered with a minister. This partnership
relationship is sacred, and that is holy.

Partnership in the work of the Lord is a sacred covenant. God
sends someone with a call and a purpose. When they answer
that call, we partner with that calling and ministry, and things
begin to happen.

15

ANGELS: OUR DIVINE HELPERS

What God has planned for you is greater than what you have planned for yourself.

In this chapter, I want to examine the work of angels, our divine helpers. Let's look at how angels were involved with Abraham:

> And the LORD appeared unto him [Abraham] in the plains of Mamre: and he sat in the tent door in the heat of the day; And he lift up his eyes and looked, and, lo, three men stood by him: and when he saw them, he ran to meet them from the tent door, and bowed himself toward the ground (Genesis 18:1-2).

Here we find the Lord—not just an angel, but the Lord, Himself—meeting Abraham to announce that Sarah would have a son. Scripture says three men came to Abraham, and that would be the Lord and two angels.

Those same two angels remained with the Lord when Abraham bargained with Him to save Sodom and Gomorrah, starting at fifty righteous and plummeting down to ten righteous persons before God would destroy the cities.

There were also two angels sent to rescue Lot and bring judgment on those cities (Genesis 19). These verses reveal the power of the angels. The Bible says angels brought judgment resulting in the destruction of Sodom and Gomorrah.

What I want you to see is that these accounts represent a unique and significant manifestation of God. Jesus came to live among man when He was born of Mary in Bethlehem. However, there are places in the Old Testament where the pre-Calvary Christ appeared to men. This story is one of those times. There are two other places in the Bible where the Lord appeared before this took place—Genesis chapters 7 and 12. The appearance in Genesis chapters 18 and 19 is different in that we have the Lord appearing with angels. A *Christophany* is an appearance of the Christ. A *theophany* is an appearance or manifestation of God.

In Genesis chapter 18, we find Abraham's promise reconfirmed by God through a Christophany that he would have a son. Some 24 years had passed since the original promise. She is 90 years old, and Abraham is 99. It was the Lord that said, *"I am going to come to you, and in the right season, very soon you are going to have a son."* Sarah laughed about it; she thought it comical. Who knows what's behind a laugh? You would laugh, too, but Sarah denied it. God called her on it and said, "Nay; but thou didst laugh" (Genesis 18:15b).

That laugh comes from the frustration of receiving a promise and still waiting after 24 years with nothing to show for it. You are undoubtedly beyond childbearing years. You are getting older and older and older, and you wonder if you ever heard from God in the first place. Was there any real validity to the word we thought we heard? It was moving when God spoke it, but let's be realistic today. That is why you laugh.

In these passages of Scripture, you have an appearance of the Lord Jesus and a visitation of angelic beings. Our focus here is on the angelic beings that came into Abraham's life.

Angels are involved in our lives, too. Sometimes we know it, and sometimes we don't. In this case, he knew it. The Bible tells us in the book of Hebrews to be careful in entertaining strangers; you might be entertaining angels. You might not even be aware of it. We probably all have had encounters with angels considering that God took the time to mention this in Scripture. I have heard people give testimonies of individuals rescued by someone who just shows up on the scene, but moments later, the person is gone. Maybe it was an angel! I don't know, but it is not farfetched and certainly not outside the confines of Scripture.

Angels Are Not People.

An angel is not a person. There is some flawed theology that says people become angels when they die—which is not surprising since sometimes our theology comes from TV shows. It's just not biblical. Angels are created in a class of their own, while humans are made in a separate class.

ESTABLISHING THE COVENANT

God's instruction to Abraham was to walk before Him and be perfect (Genesis 17:1). When we see the word "perfect," we panic because if God requires perfection from us, we're all in trouble—and we know it. So, when we read words like "perfect," it gives us some theological pause. It's like, I don't even know how to think about being perfect because I know I am far from being there.

There was no confusion about Abraham's ability toward perfection. God knew precisely that Abraham was a man just like we are and would not be perfect. God was setting the covenant in place. For the covenant to be fulfilled, there had to be one person walk perfectly before God because He said, *"I make my covenant with you and your Seed."*

The book of Galatians explains:

> Now the promises (covenants, agreements) were decreed and made to Abraham and his Seed (his Offspring, his Heir). He [God] does not say, And to seeds (descendants, heirs), as if referring to many persons, but, And to your Seed (your Descendant, your Heir), obviously referring to one individual, Who is [none other than] Christ (the Messiah) (Galatians 3:16, AMPC).

So, when God told Abraham to be perfect, He was actually speaking to the Christ. God knew that Abraham wasn't capable of being perfect. However, He knew there would be One that could walk perfectly, which was the requirement to fulfill the covenant. The fulfillment of the Abrahamic covenant was fulfilled in the One who would be perfect.

In a covenant, there are often exchanges made. You do this, and I'll do that. For God to provide the sacrificial lamb—the lamb that was slain before the foundation of the world—He had to give us His only begotten Son. When God told Abraham to give his son, He said that to bind Himself by covenant to give His Son. It was not God being mean to Abraham; it was God setting the terms of the covenant.

Genesis 22 includes the story when Abraham was called on by God to offer up his son. It says He tested Abraham, and Abraham fulfilled that mission by having every intention of offering up Isaac as a sacrifice to the Lord. He assured his son, "My son, God will provide himself a lamb for a burnt offering" (Genesis 22:8a).

This moment was awkward for both father and son. As for Isaac, he had to feel a bit nervous when he realized they were going to offer a sacrifice, and he saw no lamb. The story continues:

> And they came to the place which God had told him of; and Abraham built an altar there, and laid the wood in order, and bound Isaac his son, and laid him on the altar upon the wood. And Abraham stretched forth his hand, and took the knife to slay his son (Genesis 22:9-10).

They came to the place of sacrifice, built an altar, and laid the wood on it. It's critical to note verse 10 which says, "Abraham stretched forth his hand and took the knife to slay his son." He had every intention of going through with it.

> And the angel of the Lord called unto him out
> of heaven, and said, Abraham, Abraham: and
> he said, Here am I. And he said, Lay not thine
> hand upon the lad, neither do thou any thing
> unto him: for now I know that thou fearest
> God, seeing thou hast not withheld thy son,
> thine only son from me (Genesis 22:11-12).

Since Abraham offered his son, God was obligated to offer His Son. However, an angel stopped Abraham's hand, and because of that, their destiny was absolutely impacted by the intervention of an angelic being.

> And the angel of the Lord called unto Abraham
> out of heaven the second time, And said, By
> myself have I sworn, saith the Lord, for because
> thou hast done this thing, and hast not withheld
> thy son, thine only son: That in blessing I will
> bless thee, and in multiplying I will multiply thy
> seed as the stars of the heaven, and as the sand
> which is upon the sea shore; and thy seed shall
> possess the gate of his enemies; And in thy seed
> shall all the nations of the earth be blessed;
> because thou hast obeyed my voice (Genesis
> 22:15-18).

The angel stopped Abraham, and in that process, brought the blessing of God to him. The angel was a carrier of God's word and God's blessing. He said, *"I will bless thee and multiply thee. Your seed will be as the stars."* God reiterated and reconfirmed His promises, but it came through the intervention of an angel.

ANGELIC ASSIGNMENT

The word "angel" in and of itself means messenger. Angels are messengers of the Lord and do things in our lives, often surreptitiously. They sometimes visit us without us knowing of their presence. It is important to talk about angels because what you believe determines what you get out of life.

Let's look at a verse in Hebrews, "But to which of the angels said he at any time, Sit on my right hand, until I make thine enemies thy footstool?" (Hebrews 1:13). There is a question mark at the end of the verse signaling a rhetorical question. The answer is none; God did not say that to the angels. There is an understood answer for that verse.

The thought continues in the next verse, "Are they not all ministering spirits, sent forth to minister for them who shall be heirs of salvation?" (Hebrews 1:14). The word "minister" means servant. That is not a derogatory term. It is not a term we should look down upon or have any pious notion about angels and how they work.

The point here is that angels are not in the same class or category as humans, and they are certainly not in the same class as the Lord Jesus. They are different, and they are created for distinct reasons and diverse purposes. They have different assignments and missions.

Angels can sin, but once they do, they cannot be redeemed. If you will remember, a third of the angels fell from grace with satan. If a person sins, they have the opportunity for redemption. The blood of Jesus was shed for humans, but not for angels.

Scripture asks, "Are they not all ministering spirits, sent forth…" (Hebrews 1:14a). The phrase "sent forth" is past tense. That means they have been *sent forth* or *sent forward*. Everything necessary to do the will of God and execute the plan of God has been sent ahead. The purpose of God has already been sent forth. God does not have to send more angels; they have already been given the assignment.

Every angel needed to help you accomplish what God called you to do has already been sent ahead. You don't need a new commissioning unless you get a new assignment.

To whom are angels sent? Hebrews 1:14 goes on to answer this question by asking, "Are they not all ministering spirits, sent forth to minister for them who shall be heirs of salvation?" Look closely; it does not say minister *to*; it says to minister *for*. That is a significant difference. Who are the heirs of salvation? **YOU** are an heir of salvation now; this references your future glory in the presence of God—you are not there yet. Therefore, they have already been sent forth to minister for them who shall be. So, you do not have to wait until you get to heaven before it happens.

Angels are sent forth to minister for those who are the heirs of salvation. They are on assignment, assigned to you to help you get to your destination in one piece, having fulfilled God's will for your life.

Let's look at the following verse, which reads:

> "Therefore we ought to give the more earnest heed
> to the things which we have heard, lest at any time
> we should let them slip" (Hebrews 2:1).

The word "therefore" in this verse is a connecting word, which connects what the author said to what he is getting ready to say. In other words, the mission of angels ministering for the heirs of salvation leads immediately into the next chapter, which admonishes us not to let the things we just heard slip from our lives.

> For if the **word spoken by angels** was steadfast, and every transgression and disobedience received a just recompense of reward; How shall we escape, if we neglect so great salvation; which at the first began to be spoken by the Lord, and was confirmed unto us by them that heard him; (Hebrews 2:2-3, emphasis added).

This passage begins by mentioning words spoken by angels. He did not change the subject; the author did not start a new topic. He is still talking to us about angels.

Of course, we reference salvation in God, but the context of this is the salvation brought about from ministering spirits. What do I mean? They are not your savior; angels are not going to save you from your sins.

The word "salvation" is not just saved by grace so you can go to heaven; in many cases, it is also translated as *deliverance*—to be set free from things that take you off track or bring harm to you. Paul said you can be delivered from wicked and unruly men (2 Thessalonians 3:2), which has nothing to do with your salvation as far as going to heaven is concerned. However, it does have something to do with your success now. "Deliverance" is a common theme when discussing salvation; but, He is talking about ministering spirits that have been sent forth.

How shall we escape if we neglect what they were sent to do for us? Not just sent to us, but sent for us. Those ministering spirits have been assigned to you for the purpose of fulfilling your calling and mission and the plan of God on this earth. We simply cannot get it done without that help. All this is available through the shed blood of Jesus Christ, and none of it works without it.

> God also bearing them witness, both with signs and wonders, and with diverse miracles, and gifts of the Holy Ghost, according to his own will? **For unto the angels** hath he not put in subjection the world to come, whereof we speak (Hebrews 2:4-5, emphasis added).

Look at the bold part of the above passage: "For unto the angels..." The subject is still angels. In other words, the angels were not given authority over heaven; you were.

Let's continue reading this passage of Scripture, maintaining the subject of these verses is speaking of angels:

> But one in a certain place testified, saying, What is man, that thou art mindful of him? or the son of man that thou visitest him? Thou madest him a little lower than the angels; thou crownedst him with glory and honour, and didst set him over the works of thy hands: Thou hast put all things in subjection under his feet. For in that he put all in subjection under him, he left nothing that is not put under him. But now we see not yet all things put under him (Hebrews 2:6-8).

This passage above begins by saying, "But one in a certain place testified." Who is the one testifying? This is not a trick question. The answer is an angel. How do we know that? The "certain place" noted here is an exact quote from Psalm 8:4-6. This is an angel saying this. Let's read this quote from Psalms in context:

> O Lord, our Lord, how excellent is thy name in all the earth! who hast set thy glory above the heavens. Out of the mouth of babes and sucklings hast thou ordained strength because of thine enemies, that thou mightest still the enemy and the avenger. When I consider thy heavens, the work of thy fingers, the moon and the stars, which thou hast ordained; What is man, that thou art mindful of him? and the son of man, that thou visitest him? For thou hast made him a little lower than the angels, and hast crowned him with glory and honour. Thou madest him to have dominion over the works of thy hands; thou hast put all things under his feet: All sheep and oxen, yea, and the beasts of the field; The fowl of the air, and the fish of the sea, and whatsoever passeth through the paths of the seas. O Lord our Lord, how excellent is thy name in all the earth! (Psalm 8:1-9).

The angels witnessed God's original creation. They watched God as He declared, *"Light be!"*—and observed the creation of it. They watched the separation of the land from the sea—the fishes, birds, and creeping things. They watched as all of that was coming to completion.

After witnessing all the other grand and miraculous things, when man was created, an angel asked:

> "What is man, that thou art mindful of him? or the son of man, that thou visitest him? For thou hast made him a little lower than the angels..." (Psalm 8:4-5).

However, the exact translation for verse five is, "For thou hast made him a little lower than *God*." This is an angel saying this. In other words, this angel knew that this man had been created above him. Look at this translation in the American Standard Version:

> "For thou hast made him but little lower than **God**, And crownest him with glory and honor" (Psalm 8:5, ASV, emphasis added).

Angels are stronger in power and ability than we are, but we have a greater authority in Jesus' name than they have. This the reason they are sent forth to minister for those who are heirs of salvation.

Let's return to Hebrews, chapter two :

> But one in a certain place testified, saying, What is man, that thou art mindful of him? or the son of man that thou visitest him? Thou madest him a little lower than the angels; thou crownedst him with glory and honour, and didst set him over the works of thy hands: Thou hast put all things in subjection under his feet. For in that he put all in subjection under

him, he left nothing that is not put under him. But now we see not yet all things put under him (Hebrews 2:6-8).

The angel recognized man's authority. Man was created above the angels. Sin dropped us down below them, but we were initially created above them. When you are in Jesus, you receive back your position of authority over the angels.

But we see Jesus, who was made a little lower than the angels for the suffering of death, crowned with glory and honour; that he by the grace of God should taste death for every man (Hebrews 2:9).

The Bible says we are looking through a glass darkly (1 Corinthians 13:12); we can't see everything clearly. We do not know all over which we have control, and you will only find out what through the New Covenant. We gained it all back the day we made Jesus Christ the Lord of our lives. We just did not know we had it, and the devil wants to keep us ignorant.

When you walk in ignorance and darkness, you are neglecting your great salvation. You will still go to heaven, but you have ignored the authority that God gave you, and you will not fulfill your destiny until you know this. I am talking to you about cooperating with your destiny. You have a destiny and a future, but will you get there? My answer to that question is that you will get there if you know how to do it.

As Christians, we must call on those angels because they are sent to minister for us; they are available to help us. You must have supernatural help in the spiritual world out there that you cannot see. In the invisible realm, there are not only angels out there; there are other entities at work also. We call on the Lord first because He gives us the authority we need, but we use that authority to call on the angels to aid us.

Who you gonna call?
I'm calling on Jesus! Not Ghostbusters!

16

ANGELS: OUR PROTECTORS

Psalm 91 tells us that angels bear us up and protect us:

> For he shall give his angels charge over thee, to keep thee in all thy ways. They shall bear thee up in their hands, lest thou dash thy foot against a stone. Thou shalt tread upon the lion and adder: the young lion and the dragon shalt thou trample under feet. Because he hath set his love upon me, therefore will I deliver him: I will set him on high, because he hath known my name. He shall call upon me, and I will answer him: I will be with him in trouble; I will deliver him, and honour him. With long life will I satisfy him, and shew him my salvation (Psalm 91:11-16).

This Bible passage says that angels protect us. The word "keep" is like a gatekeeper, a doorkeeper, or someone who has been given something to keep safe. It is a word that declares protection and safety—a keeping place, a safe, or a strongbox. You put something in there for safekeeping.

Let's focus on verses 11 and 12 and look at them from the Living Bible to get a better understanding:

> For he orders his angels to protect you wherever you go. They will steady you with their hands to keep you from stumbling against the rocks on the trail (Psalm 91:11-12, TLB).

SPEAK THE WORD OF GOD

You have angelic protection even when you don't realize it; they bear you up in their hands. It is a miracle for you to live out your days on this planet, much less to do anything with them. Just to keep on showing up and finishing life is a big deal. Human life is fragile. There are all kinds of things that can take you out. We need help.

However, God wants you to know that **you are not alone**. He did not put you here alone; He gave you some helpers. But how shall you escape if you neglect those that God has given you to help you fulfill your mission?

Look at another passage in the book of Psalms:

> Bless the Lord, ye his angels, that excel in strength, that do his commandments, hearkening unto the voice of his word. Bless ye the Lord, all ye his hosts; ye ministers of his, that do his pleasure (Psalm 103:20-21).

This passage describes what happens when you pay attention to the responsibility that you have with your angels. The angels excel in strength, and they hearken to or heed the voice of the Word of God. God tells them what to do, and they do it.

When your Bible is open, you have a lap full of the Word of God, ready and waiting. You have the voice of God beckoning from two feet away. God's Word coming from your mouth has the same power as the Word of God coming from God's mouth. You are the body of Christ.

> For verily I say unto you, That whosoever shall say unto this mountain, Be thou removed, and be thou cast into the sea; and shall not doubt in his heart, **but shall believe that those things which he saith shall come to pass; he shall have whatsoever he saith** (Mark 11:23, emphasis added).

The Bible tells us to speak to the mountain; it did not say that God would speak to it. It said that if **you** would say to the mountain and not doubt, it would obey you. So, **your words** are the ones that put the mountain in the sea. God's Word has already said it, but it will not work for you until it comes from your mouth. Angels have already been sent, but they do nothing for you when you are in conflict with what God said.

When you say things like, *"Oh, I'm so fearful. I guess I'm just going to go broke. We never get ahead. Nothing goes right for me."* That is certainly not the faith-filled voice of the Word of God moving out in the earth. When you say things like this, you have given in to something in absolute conflict with your purpose and destiny. At that point, you are licensing your destiny to be trampled underfoot by your unbelief and by your words.

Because you are in conflict with what God says about you, you cannot get your angels to act on your behalf. God wants you to employ your angels and get them to work. When some people hear this truth, they mistakenly think, *"I want my angels to go to the kitchen and get me a glass of water."* That is not how it works; we are not talking about that kind of service. Angels are not that kind of servant. We are talking about the spirit world where there is a war raging. Through Jesus and His authority, you have victory in that war swirling around you, and you can walk through this world unscathed. These angels are at work for you.

Let's look at Psalm 103 from a different translation:

> Bless the Lord, you mighty angels of his who carry out his orders, listening for each of his commands. Yes, bless the Lord, you armies of his angels who serve him constantly (Psalm 103:20-21, TLB).

These angels are the group referred to in the King James Version as "ye ministers of his, that do his pleasure" (Psalm 103:21, KJV). God's pleasure is to minister to you or for you when you give voice to the Word of God. You are God's agent in the earth; He has no one else. You are the body of Christ; there is not another one. Some may respond, *"I'm waiting on someone else to do it."* Sorry, but it is not going to happen that way. You're it.

Angels hearken to the voice of God's Word. When we talk about our unbelief, doubts, fears, and failures, we subsequently bind the powers sent to assist us. Those sent to work for you will not actually work against you; they just stand idle and refuse to work at all.

There are enough demonic forces out there working against you; you don't need more. I want to emphasize in the strongest way imaginable: **you cannot keep demons at bay without the help of angels.** When you use the name of Jesus, the angels' ears perk up and listen. Many times, we give our angels nothing at all with which to work.

We must give angels the Word of God. We must speak the truth; we must pray. We must do things to put our authority to use—exercise it. Angels are our ministering spirits, and when we don't give them anything to do, we neglect our helpers, our rescuers, and our ministers. How shall we escape if we neglect or ignore that ministry?

THE REALM OF ANGELS

In the Bible, we can see an example of how an angel materialized to some apostles:

> Then the high priest rose up, and all they that were with him, (which is the sect of the Sadducees,) and were filled with indignation, And laid their hands on the apostles, and put them in the common prison. But the angel of the Lord by night opened the prison doors, and brought them forth, and said, Go, stand and speak in the temple to the people all the words of this life (Acts 5:17-20).

They were in prison, but the angel of the Lord opened the cell doors. The angel physically came and opened them. When you mention angels to some, they think in terms of a celestial being floating around. No, in this case, a physical angel stood there and actually opened a tangible door.

Angels live in the realm above the speed of light, but you live in a realm that functions well below light speed. That is why you can't see them, even though they are just as real as you are. However, you can have a manifestation of an angel when needed. That is how we could possibly entertain them unknowingly.

When matter moves beyond the speed of light, it becomes invisible. Einstein's *Theory of Relativity* says if you speed up matter to the point of being faster than the speed of light, two things happen: time slows down or stops, and the matter in question becomes invisible. It is important to note that things do not cease to exist; they just become invisible.

For example, Jesus came into a room without opening the door—He passed through it. After the resurrection, Jesus accelerated beyond the speed of light but then decelerated below it so we could see Him. That is a simple explanation of how it works. We cannot see or detect that realm, but it is there, nonetheless.

Some have seen angels, and some have not. You don't have to see them for them to be at work. Often, we are probably hearing them and don't recognize them for who they are.

While I have been preaching a sermon, credible people in the congregation have told me they saw a giant angel eight or nine feet tall standing beside me. They usually say something like, *"He was talking to you while you preached. He would tell you something, and then you repeated it aloud."* I have had that happen dozens of times, and it is almost always the same story. I have never seen it, but I believe it. Angels are messengers to the church.

Faith Frames Your World

The Bible says the worlds were framed by the Word of God and by faith. The Bible says that faith is the substance of things hoped for and the evidence of things not seen.

> Now faith is the assurance (the confirmation, the title deed) of the things [we] hope for, being the proof of things [we] do not see and the conviction of their reality [faith perceiving as real fact what is not revealed to the senses] (Hebrews 11:1, AMPC).

People say that the worlds were flung into existence from nothing, but that is not true. They were hurled into existence and formed by a substance called faith. Faith is the substance of that realm. You cannot see or touch it, but faith will change your life.

Faith is representative of the Play-Doh™ that we played with as children. We molded it and made models of all sorts of things. In the spirit realm, we mold and create things with faith by our words. That is what God did. He formed the world through faith, through His words.

If you are financially broke, don't talk about it. If you do not have any money, talk about God's prosperity. That is how you change it; build the model you want.

Angels in Action

In Acts 12, Peter was locked up in prison. When he was thrown into the prison, an angel came and loosed his chains and opened the prison doors. Let's read about it from the Bible:

193

And suddenly an angel of the Lord approached him, and a light shone in the prison. He struck Peter on the side and woke him up, saying, "Rise up, quickly." And the chains fell off his hands. Then the angel said to him, "Dress yourself and put your sandals on." And he did so. Then he said to him, "Wrap your cloak around you and follow me." He went out and followed him, and did not know that what was done by the angel was real, but thought he was seeing a vision. When they had passed the first and the second guards, they came to the iron gate leading to the city, which opened to them by itself. And they went out and went forward one street. And immediately the angel left him. When Peter had come to himself, he said, "Now I certainly know that the Lord has sent His angel and delivered me from the hand of Herod and from all that the Jewish people were expecting" (Acts 12:7-11, MEV).

You can also see how the angels were at work for Daniel in the lion's den:

Then the king arose very early in the morning and went in haste to the den of lions. When he came to the den, he cried with a voice full of sorrow to Daniel. And the king spoke and said to Daniel, "Daniel, servant of the living God, has your God whom you serve continually been able to deliver you from the lions?" Then Daniel said to the king, "O king, live forever! My God has sent His angel and has shut the lions' mouths so that they have not hurt me, because innocence was found in me before Him; and also before you, O king, I have done no harm." Then the king was exceeding glad for him and commanded that they take Daniel up out of the den. So Daniel was taken up out of the den, and no manner of harm was found on him, because he believed in his God (Daniel 6:19-23, MEV).

When Daniel was in the lion's den, the Bible says that God sent an angel to shut the lion's mouths. If Daniel had not been a man of faith and had not believed God, he would not have fulfilled his destiny.

Another example is the three Hebrew children in a burning fiery furnace. An angel was sent from God, and they came out of that furnace and did not even smell like smoke! That is what angels do.

Satan wants to take you out. He will take you out with a hangnail if he can get by with it; the enemy will use anything he can. The Bible did not say that the devil came just to harass you, even though he will surely do that. No, his goal is to steal, kill, and destroy you. He does not want merely to damage you; he wants to wipe you out. So, why can't he? Because Christians have access to angels, the power of God, and the name of Jesus!

Remember in Acts 27, when Paul was on that boat in a major tropical storm? He was violently tossed about on that ship for days upon days. The Bible says, "For there stood by me this night the angel of God, whose I am, and whom I serve" (Acts 27:23). An angel of God stood by Paul and told him that the ship would be lost, but all would be saved if they remained with

COOPERATING WITH YOUR DESTINY

him. They were not going to fulfill their destiny if they got away from him. The entire crew was delivered because of Paul's presence. That is a good word if you are going to travel somewhere on an airplane. All the passengers, especially the unbelievers, should be glad you are on that flight.

12 THINGS ANGELS WILL DO FOR YOU

Here are 12 things that angels do for you that come straight from the Bible.

1) **Angels bring us messages from God.** Those angels in Revelation, chapters two and three, were messengers from God to the church.

2) **They warn us of danger.** Remember Lot's story? The angel said, *"Lot, get out of Sodom; something is coming!"*

3) **They guard us against evil.** Daniel, Shadrach, Meshach, and Abednego were protected from the fiery furnace.

4) **They strengthen us when we are tempted.** The angels came to Jesus and ministered to Him when He was on the Mount of Temptation.

5) **They bring instructions to us from God.** Just like they did with Moses on Mount Sinai.

6) **They rescue us from trouble.** We have seen that with Peter, Paul, Daniel, and others.

7) **They encourage us when it is needed.** Do you ever need encouragement? God has angels that become your encouragers as He did for Joseph, Mary, and Zacharias.

8) **They guide us in life.** In Acts 8:26, the angel told Philip to go south. Angels will guide you in your life.

9) **They prosper your life.** The Bible says the angel of the Lord went before Abraham's servant to prosper all his ways or prosper him in the way (Genesis 24:40). Dollars and cents are not the only definitions of prosperity. If you do not listen to the angel of the Lord, you probably will not be as prosperous as God wants you to be.

10) **They guard little children.**

Take heed that ye despise not one of these little ones; for I say unto you, That in heaven their angels do always behold the face of my Father which is in heaven (Matthew 18:10).

11) **They carry us to heaven when we die.** Do you remember the beggar? The Bible says the angels carried him into Abraham's bosom (Luke 16:22).

On two occasions, I've seen angels in the room when someone was dying, and people were holding on to them in prayer because they didn't want them to die. The angels were focused entirely on the sick person. They were not the least bit interested in all the commotion going on around the room. I saw the dead person's spirit leave their body. When their spirit floated up, those angels ascended with the person, and their heads went through the ceiling. The angels stayed exactly level with the person leaving their body. I didn't hear about it or read about it in a book; I saw it. I haven't seen that event many times, but I have seen it twice.

12) **They nourish us in our time of need.** Hagar and her son were sent away. The water had run out, and in a time of anguish and hopelessness, an angel revealed her purpose and showed her water to drink (Genesis 21). Angels become the supply.

Angels are God's messengers that excel in strength. Angels are on your side to help you in life. They are sent to prosper you on your journey. They are always present with you and will take you to your destiny. We are to acknowledge that angels are sent from God, but we don't worship them. As we speak the Word and use the name of Jesus, we are enabled to loose or release them on behalf of their assignment for God's destiny and purpose in our lives.

17

YOUR IDENTITY AFFECTS YOUR DESTINY

Destiny is one of those subjects that we hear a lot about, not only in the church world, but also in society. In this chapter, we are going to talk about how your identity affects your destiny.

Abraham was a man that went out in pursuit of God, not knowing where he was going. Throughout that pursuit, we see that many things he faced are often things we have to deal with in our lives today.

Scripture tells us that Abraham is the father of our faith.

The Bible asks: whose faith do you follow? According to the Scripture, we should follow the very clear example God gave us in Abraham. He walked in his purpose, even with the many challenges he faced along the way. Abraham fulfilled his destiny.

Let's look at Abraham's life more closely:

"And when Abram was ninety years old and nine, the LORD appeared to Abram, and said unto him, I am the Almighty God; walk before me, and be thou perfect" (Genesis 17:1).

A Name Change

We have talked some about this, but I want to draw your attention to it again as we go forward. According to this verse, Abraham was 99 years old when God spoke to him here. However, when God first began talking to him in Genesis 12, he was 75 years old. It was at that point when he started to go toward the place God had prepared for him—the place God had created for him. We are calling it his destiny.

Twenty-four years elapsed between the time God gave Abraham his first promise and this moment in chapter 17. Here we find God appearing to him again, saying, "And I will make my covenant between me and thee, and will multiply thee exceedingly" (Genesis 17:2).

God is renewing and reiterating His call on Abraham and reassuring him that He is involved in what Abraham is doing.

> And Abram fell on his face: and God talked with him, saying, As for me, behold, my covenant is with thee, and thou shalt be a father of many nations. Neither shall thy name any more be called Abram, but thy name shall be Abraham; for a father of many nations have I made thee (Genesis 17:3-5).

It's been twenty-four years since the promise came, and here God visited Abram, again saying, *"I want to change your name. When you tell someone who you are, or when someone calls your name, I don't want them to call you Abram; I want your new name to be spoken: Abraham—father of many nations."*

The word "Abraham" means **the father of a multitude.** God marked Abraham in a way that was consistent with his destiny. God changed his identity; Abram was now Abraham. This is not arbitrary; changing someone's name is something you see God do a few times in Scripture.

THE CALL

A "dog tag" is issued by the military to every soldier under their authority. The main reason they distribute those tags is to help them correctly identify you in the event of your death.

Your identity is what identifies or describes you. That is what God was doing with Abraham in these passages. He was changing Abraham's identity to adjust how he established himself. God wanted Abraham to see himself in a certain way, and He wanted every word spoken to him about who he was to reflect what God had called him to do.

God changed Abram's name to Abraham, the father of a multitude. Whenever someone called his name, there was a declaration being made about his destiny—I am the father of a multitude. At that time, Abraham did not even have a child with Sarah yet. His destiny determined what God **called** him.

We often refer to a person's "call"—the calling of God. The gifts and callings of God are without repentance or are not revokable (Romans 11:29). We talk about the call into the ministry or the call to do something specific.

Sometimes we have somewhat of an abstract understanding of the word "calling." It becomes so vague and murky that it is beyond our ability to comprehend; it's out there in the ether somewhere. That is true to a degree because it is supernatural, and it does take place in the spirit. At the same time, I do not think your calling is as mysterious or incomprehensible as that.

There are people in the Bible called to be prophets, pastors, or teachers; however, some are called to do it all. If you have a destiny in God, that call from God is your destiny.

When I was a little boy, I would typically play outside until dark. I would only come home when my mother called me. She would come to the back door and call out my name. It was an amazing thing; she never called me Ralph. Why? Because I wouldn't have responded to her because I'm not Ralph, I'm Eddie. How amazing that my mother would always call me by my name. When God calls you something, that is absolutely what He intends for you to be—what He intends for you to do with your life. However, we have difficulty relating to Abraham's call and look at it as something mysterious.

God called Jeremiah a prophet; He called Paul an apostle; He called Peter a rock. When He calls you something, it is His destiny for you. We don't need to be too nervous about this concept of "the call." It is God who calls us, which means He speaks something over us or to us. What He speaks over us is what we were created to be, and because He spoke it, everything in the universe must line up with it.

To cooperate with your destiny, you must acknowledge what He speaks to you—that's your part. God is the only one who can do the calling. You can't call yourself; He calls you. But when He calls you, you must agree with the calling.

I know of a teenager named Mary that some say was 15 years old or so when visited by an angel and told she was highly favored. The angel said God had called her to give birth to His Son. Her response was, "Be it unto me according to thy word" (Luke 1:38).

Notice that she had to cooperate with the call, but she did not initiate it. Her destiny was not hers to choose from a large group. It was not like a fruit tree out in the backyard that you pick off what you want. The spiritual calling is divinely given and spoken by God, and we must cooperate with it.

YOUR CALL IDENTIFIES YOU

Our identity is related to what we do with the name God calls us. There is a work associated with it, but I want to focus more on the name He calls us. God called Abram "Abraham" because that name was a fulfillment of what he was called to do.

Let's look at how the Lord dealt with Sarai. The Bible says, "And God said unto Abraham, As for Sarai thy wife, thou shalt not call her name Sarai, but Sarah shall her name be" (Genesis 17:15). Not only did God change Abram's name to *Abraham*, but He also changed Sarai's name to *Sarah*, meaning "princess or queen." In this name change, God put a call on her life; He called her to a specific thing as well.

Your identity is how you distinguish yourself in relationship to how God sees you, and it has everything to do with your destiny.

We know that God visited Abraham on several occasions to confirm what he was called to do. God gave this couple a new identity because He wanted to change how they identified themselves or with what they identified.

Your identity is what distinguishes you from another; it gives you a sense of self and self-worth. If we talk to someone in a casual conversation, one of the first things we ask is their name and what they do. Immediately, we relate their identity with what they do. People say: *I am Christy, and I am a doctor. I'm Ed, and I'm a pastor. I'm Peyton, I used to be an NFL quarterback, but now I sell pizzas.* We identify not only the person, but we identify the person with what they do. Your identity makes you unique; you are not just like everyone else. Once you have an identity, it separates you.

When my mother called my name, it separated me from all the other kids in the neighborhood that were outside playing. When she called my name, I knew to respond. None of the other kids responded because their names had not been called. Your name identifies, separates, and describes you in a very real sense.

Our destiny is an unfolding revelation. What God began in Abraham at age 75 was not fully revealed; He still reveals more even when Abraham is 99. However, there was a beginning—a start.

At the beginning of your walk with God, there were certain things He spoke to you as well; however, as you continue to make progress with the Lord, things begin to change and alter—more is revealed, but accomplishments up to that point are not nullified. Other things are added because we build line upon line, frame upon frame, foundation upon foundation. We build a life; we build a future.

You are more capable as you get older than you were when you started. Hopefully, you have learned enough that you do not continue to make some of the mistakes you made early on. We grow up and are more experienced. We become more able because we know more than before.

We not only know more than we used to know; hopefully, we also get smarter than we used to be. Not just more knowledge, but utilizing more wisdom as we grow in God. Knowledge and wisdom are not one and the same. You can have a great amount of knowledge with no wisdom, and you are just an educated fool. Knowledge alone does not give you the ability to accomplish your destiny, and wisdom needs to have some knowledge added to it.

The book of Ecclesiastes gives us an example of a poor wise man that no one listened to. As long as he remained a poor wise man—incapable of applying it to his own life—nobody paid any attention to him (Ecclesiastes 9).

We initially get on our path in God, but we make lots of discoveries along the way. Consequently, what was good at 75, hopefully gets enhanced in the coming years—by the time you are 99 in this case.

SARAH'S LAUGH

We touched on Sarah's laugh in an earlier chapter, but let's revisit it. Imagine the thoughts that went through their minds: Abraham at ninety-nine, and Sarah at ninety! Can you imagine what they were thinking concerning God's promises and how unlikely it was—naturally speaking—for them to come to pass? Truly, it seemed like a joke; it seemed like some ridiculous bad joke. When the Lord and those two angels reconfirmed Abraham's promise and announced Sarah would have a son, she laughed. She thought, *"Are you kidding me right now?"* In this situation with Sarah, you have a 24-year-old promise that had not yet been fulfilled. You also had a false attempt to fulfill the will of God through Ishmael, and that didn't work. Think of how you would feel if you were her. Do you think you would laugh?

Could it be? The Lord manifested here to speak to her; it was not just Uncle Joe down at the convenience store speaking. No, this is the Lord saying she will have a son. This promise had been so elusive and drawn out over 24 years; Sarah just laughed.

The stark reality of her situation begins to settle in when you think through the process she endured—the joy and laughter that comes from the original promise, then having waited and believed for 24 years without anything happening. And then, BAM! There is the promise again! Hope turns to cynicism. That's the type of laugh she had.

That is also the kind of laugh you would probably have if you were in a similar spot. The hope of what you thought would never happen is promised, but the delay year after year dashes your joy. What was a joyous thing at one time has now turned into promises. Sarah could have said, *"Promises. Promises. All I get are promises. Just don't give me any more promises."* That is the laugh.

I hate to say it, but we probably have all laughed that laugh. You see something you have been standing for a long time— God's destiny or promise—and it's been just out of your reach. You feel like: *I was believing, but look what has happened.* Then, you get to the point where hope becomes despair and hopelessness. In this light, your outlook turns cynical, and you say, *"Yeah, I'd love it. But I've felt this way before and look where I am now."* We may have felt that way, but faith presses on.

GOD WILL FULFILL HIS PROMISE

Let me be clear here: Anything that God has promised you, He intends to fulfill it just like He said. He is not playing games with you; He is serious about it. There's a destiny in God that He has for you even if it has been evasive, elusive—looking like it's never going to happen. I am here to tell you **it is going to happen.** Just hold steady.

When the fowls come to steal the sacrifice and dark times come, and you don't know what to do, just hold steady to the promise. Watch and see. God, who parted the Red Sea, is the same God that will do for you what He promised. Do you think you can't get healed? I have news for you. God is a healing God. And what He said about you He intends to bring to pass.

Some may say, *"But it's been elusive. It's evaded me. It's not working."* I'm telling you: don't stop believing. Don't give away that giddy hope of your first response, and don't let cynicism set in and take away all your ability to believe. Do not give it up; continue to believe.

God continued to encourage Abraham about His promise. Twenty-four years after the promise, God shows up and says, *"I am going to change your name and call you the father of a multitude. Oh, and by the way, I'm going to change Sarai's name as well. I am going to call her princess bride."* God would not let them quit believing.

207

When you step out like Abraham and Sarah did and continue to believe, it takes faith to fulfill your destiny. It is a test of faith. Remember that Abraham is the father of our faith. What we see him doing and going through can be inspirational to us. Guidance can come to us through it.

IT's A Process

In Jesus' first encounter with Peter and Andrew, we see this exchange:

> And Jesus, walking by the sea of Galilee, saw two brethren, Simon called Peter, and Andrew his brother, casting a net into the sea: for they were fishers. And he saith unto them, **Follow me**, and I will **make you** fishers of men (Matthew 4:18-19, emphasis added).

He said, "Follow me, and I will make you..." Notice that the **following** comes before the **making**.

When God told Abraham to leave his country for a land He would be shown, it was a "follow Me" moment. God says: *"Follow Me, and I will make you."* Twenty-four years later, God has not given up on the promise. Twenty-four years later and God is still as involved as He was on day one. Twenty-four years later and God has not forgotten any promise He made. God is making Abraham what He promised as Abraham followed Him.

God is saying that to you, too. Follow Him... and then what? He will make you. God is making us something. God is making us someone. God is making us something that fits His plan. Sometimes, however, we are not ready to be made. Why?

Maybe we have a little more work to do. You are a person in the making; we are under construction. We are being made, but it is not finished. He is the author and the finisher. What He starts, He finishes. He is the author and the finisher of our faith (Hebrews 12:2).

It is a process. Sarah and Abraham had to have an identity change before doing what God wanted them to do. Your identity will determine with what you identify. Some of us are exactly like Abraham and Sarah in that we need an identity change.

AN IDENTITY CHANGE

Maybe you came from the wrong side of the tracks or possibly from a family that did not even want you. You may have come from a place where you wrecked your life, and you were put on the ash heap. But then God reached down and touched your life. If that's you, you must have an identity change. You must see yourself differently than you saw yourself before. You have to see yourself in a way that you haven't before seen. God can help you change your identity.

Some may say, *"Well, I used to be a drug addict."* Change your identity. You may have been a lot of things. *"I came from a broken home, or I came from deep poverty."* It's imperative that you have an identity change—a total makeover.

God will change your identity just like He changed Abraham's. He's not **going to** do it; no, He **has already done** it. When God speaks about the future to us, it may not yet be visible in our world, but you are going to experience it. However, in God's economy, the promise has already been completed; His work is already done. It has been granted. Now, you must live it out.

2 Corinthians 5:17 says, "Therefore if any man be in Christ, he is a new creature: old things are passed away; behold, all things are become new." We must identify with the new creature. We cannot identify with the old man; the old man is gone. For those of us who have put on Christ Jesus, the old man is dead.

We have "put on" or identify with the new man. This new man is not a drug addict. This new man is not impoverished or purposeless. This new man is not from the dregs of the earth. This new man is not homeless, looking for a home. This new man is accepted in the beloved. This man is the righteousness of God in Christ; he is a new creation. Jesus Himself said that He was made poor that this new man might be made rich (2 Corinthians 8:9). Which man are you identifying with? Which identity are you putting on?

The world wants to drag you back to be the old man. It wants to tell you that you cannot get out of your mess. There's a country song that says, "Don't get above your raising." I am sure people said that to Abraham.

God said, *"I am doing a total identity change on you. You were that, but now you are this."* When God calls you something, He means it—and God called you a new creation. The least you can do is agree with Him.

WHEN GOD CHANGES YOUR NAME

You find over and over in the Bible where God changed people's names for various reasons: Abram became Abraham, Sarai became Sarah, and Jacob became Israel. When we hear the name of Israel today, we do not even think of the man Jacob anymore; we think of a nation of people. When God changed Jacob's name to Israel, He spoke a nation into existence. He was changing it all.

When you say "amen" or "so be it" to what God is calling you to do, He is changing your future. You are cooperating with the destiny He has for you.

Another example of a name change was when Simon Bar-Jonah, the fisherman, had his name changed to Peter, the Rock. We first see Peter as an impetuous, undisciplined person with his foot in his mouth again and again. However, after he was filled with the Holy Spirit, that same Peter stood up and preached a message on Pentecost where 3,000 souls were saved. That is what happens when you identify with what God calls you to do instead of acting like the old man.

The man Simon Bar-Jonah would from that day forward be called Peter, the Rock. Think about that—impulsive, undisciplined, unstable, unsteady, and doing things without thinking Peter. A rock? Jesus solidified his destiny in Scripture, saying, "And I say also unto thee, That thou art Peter, and upon this rock I will build my church; and the gates of hell shall not prevail against it" (Matthew 16:18).

Another example of a name change is Saul of Tarsus, who killed Christians. What did God do? He changed his name to Paul, the apostle. This man who killed Christians for their faith became the number one apostle of the New Testament. When Paul began to take his identity from God instead of identifying with his past, he gave us over half of the New Testament!

Paul thoroughly identified with the new man even after killing Christians in his early days. After his conversion, he said, *"I did it ignorantly, not knowing… I have wronged no man."* He had a thorough understanding of God's grace and application of the change that took place in him. He was not that old man any longer. That old man was gone, and a new man had taken his place.

RECEIVE YOUR IDENTITY CHANGE

When God changes your identity, He changes everything about you. When you agree with it, you are not who you used to be.

The Scripture says in Mark 6:4, "A prophet is not without honor save in his own country and around his own kinfolk." The God's Word translation says this:

> "But Jesus told them, 'The only place a prophet isn't
> honored is in his hometown, among his relatives,
> and in his own house'" (Mark 6:4, GW).

Why are you without honor at home? Because your country and the people around you want to remind you of who you were, not who you are. God reminds you of who He made you. People familiar with you will not let you prosper because you might get "above yourself." They say, *"We don't want you to get high and mighty."* Your response to them is to be confident in God without apology; we must identify with Him.

The people you know, and those you grew up with, want to remind you of who you were, not who you are.

The point is that we must change our identity to what corresponds with what God says about us. We used to be sinners, but now we are saints and new creatures. You cannot be known as a sinner anymore. Some Christians say, *"Well, I'm just an old sinner."* That's not true. You are a saint; you were saved from that old identity. You are not that old sinner anymore. You gave up that old man when you became a child of God.

We used to be bound by sin, but now we are free in Christ. We used to be sick and defeated, but now we are healed and more than conquerors. We used to be victims, and now we are victors. We used to be bound, but now we are loosed. We used to be powerless, but now we are powerful. Your destiny and identity have to match; you must choose to identify with your destiny.

COOPERATING WITH YOUR DESTINY

18

STEPPING OUT INTO YOUR DESTINY

I remember when God was dealing with me for several years about going into the ministry. The pressure would increase and intensify, and I really did not want to do it. I was happy doing something else. But I remember driving to church on a Wednesday night, and I told Nora, *"Tonight, I'm going to stand in front of that congregation and tell them that I'm called to preach. From this day forward, I will be called a preacher."* Why did I have to do that? If God called me to preach, that's what I also have to call myself.

I remember the internal struggles that went on for so long that totally disappeared the minute I publicly declared that I was called to preach. All the burden lifted and never came back. However, as long as I refused to say it or take that identity, the struggle remained. I had to accept and embrace what God had called me to do.

Even after I made my declaration, I didn't become a preacher immediately. Nothing looked like it had changed at all; in fact, everything looked exactly the same. We went back to the same house in the same car, and I went to the same job the next day. But I can tell you that **everything** began to change from that point on.

AGREE WITH GOD

When walking with God, your destiny and your identity must match. You have to agree with your identity in Christ and cooperate with your destiny. In doing this, you identify with the New Covenant.

We cannot identify with defeat and have victory. If we stay in the past, it will rob us of our destiny—our future. Satan's condemnation about your past is his attempt to keep you from fulfilling your destiny.

The apostle Paul admonished us that we are to forget the past and press into the future. It takes effort, but we must. He said:

> But this one thing I do, forgetting those things which are behind, and reaching forth unto those things which are before, I press toward the mark for the prize of the high calling of God in Christ Jesus (Philippians 3:13b-14).

Paul pressed forward to what God called him to do; he would not stop pressing. God called him as an apostle; Paul called himself an apostle. When he wrote all those letters, he said, *"I, Paul, the apostle, write unto you. I am not an apostle to others. Yea, doubtless I am to you."* He agreed with God.

Your destiny requires you to agree with God. We are to call ourselves what God calls us. God calls you healed, you must call yourself healed as well. If God calls you blessed, then you must also call yourself blessed. For you to do this, the Lord counts it as a right and honorable thing. If God calls you prosperous, then you must cooperate. If God calls you victorious, you say that. If God calls you an overcomer, then you call yourself an overcomer. To identify with defeat means we have not taken on our new identity, the new creature. We must let the past be the past.

> For you are still [unspiritual, having the nature] of the flesh [under the control of ordinary impulses]. For as long as [there are] envying and jealousy and wrangling and factions among you, are you not unspiritual and of the flesh, behaving yourselves after a human standard and like mere (unchanged) men? (1 Corinthians 3:3, AMPC).

Our identity is our destiny. When we refuse to pursue our destiny and fail to identify with what God said to us, we act like mere unchanged men. However, as Christians, you are not unchanged; you are a new creation in Christ Jesus. Through the new birth, you have encountered a major change to become a new creation.

SAY YES TO GOD

To experience our destiny, we must take on that new identity. You are what God calls you; that is your destiny. It is common courtesy to acknowledge what God says about you, but more important, it is faith in action. Accepting and agreeing with what God says is an act of faith. You have to call things the way God does for those things to be active in your life.

Some of us dodge our destiny, and some of us do not want to admit it. Just like I did, some run from it. Unfortunately, the resources of heaven will never come toward you until you say "yes" to your destiny in God. You have to say yes.

An angel told Mary that she would bear the son of the living God, but God required a "yes" from her. He was not going to make her do it; she had to say "yes." In the same way, He will not make you do anything before you say "yes" as well. You have a destiny, but you have to give yourself to it and not run from it. Trust God with your future. He is trustworthy; you can believe Him.

Mary had to embrace her calling before it happened. Jeremiah had to accept his calling to be a prophet. David had to accept the calling to be a king; he could not identify as a shepherd any longer. Moses had to accept his calling and be a leader of a nation; he had to leave the backside of the desert. You cannot hang around in the desert when you have been called to lead a nation.

Some might say they wouldn't dare voice what God has spoken to their hearts about their destiny. However, if God said something about you, you are authorized to say it. Being called by God is what gives you authority.

When we first started our church, Nora wasn't the co-pastor; she was my wife. In the world where we grew up, women could not pastor. However, people in our congregation saw the calling on her life and God's endorsement of her in that position. Now she's the co-pastor.

To cooperate, you have to say it. If God said it, you are authorized to speak it. If He didn't say it, then don't say it. You are not going to walk in what God has promised you until you say it. When you do say it, all the resources of heaven are going to come to your aid to bring it to pass. What you cannot fulfill, He will.

Sarai was crushed by the memories of those hopeless years of being barren and with no child, but God intervened to give her renewed hope. He reached out into that situation and said, *"No, Sarah, do not identify as a barren woman. You identify as a queen, a princess, the mother of a nation."*

That is what God is saying to you. Maybe not the exact words He spoke to Sarah or the same words He said to Abraham, but He is saying to you:

> *Take courage, do not be afraid, step out, do what I have called you to do. Obey My voice and watch Me do for you what you could never do for yourself. Watch Me arrange circumstances that you could never orchestrate. Watch Me put things in your path that you could never, ever imagine would be there. I will accomplish the things I have spoken to you.*

Your obedience to step out in faith is all God needs. When you cooperate with your destiny, it is just the excuse He needs to bring all of heaven's resources to you.

ABOUT THE AUTHOR

DR. ED KING has a strong prophetic calling with a strong healing anointing. He bases his beliefs and teachings on God's Word.

Dr. King is founder and senior pastor of Redemption Church in Knoxville, Tennessee, where he has served for over forty years. He is also the president of the Power of the Word television ministry, which broadcasts both nationally and internationally. In addition to traveling the world and preaching the Gospel of Jesus Christ at leadership conferences and evangelistic meetings, Dr. King is the author of eight books. He and his wife, co-pastor Nora King, make their home in Knoxville, Tennessee. Together they have one daughter, Laren, and a son, Marcus, who is in heaven.

Power of the Word Ministries
Dr. Ed King
PO Box 52466
Knoxville TN 37950 USA
1.800.956.4433
www.poweroftheword.com
info@poweroftheword.com
youtube.com/user/RedemptionChurch

Redemption Church
3550 Pleasant Ridge Rd
Knoxville TN 37921 USA
865.521.7777
www.redemptionchurch.com
info@redemptionchurch.com
youtube.com/user/RedemptionChurch

BOOKS BY NORA KING

OVERCOMING IN DIFFICULT TIMES

Based on her own experiences and biblical insight, Nora King shares practical ways to rise above the ashes of difficulty and despair. You can move from tragedy to triumph. Don't give up; rise up and live again!

ISBN: 9781602731189
152 pages

30 DAYS TO A BETTER PRAYER LIFE

In this exciting book, Nora King offers fresh revelation and practical teaching to help you experience the release of God's power. You will learn daily how to improve your prayer life and enter God's presence through these simple principles. You don't have to struggle to pray any longer!

ISBN: 9781602730120
142 pages

Parsons Publishing House
Your Voice Your World ™

Available at your local or online bookstores and www.redemptionchurch.com.

BOOKS BY DR. ED KING

WILL MY PET BE IN HEAVEN?
ISBN: 9781602730687 • 92 pages.

THE TIMING OF GOD—His Timetable for Your Life
ISBN: 978160273717 • 118 pages.

DEDICATING YOUR HOUSE
ISBN: 9781602730861 • 114 pages.

LOYALTY—Going Beyond Faithfulness
ISBN: 9781602730793 • 110 pages.

WHAT'S GOING ON?
Why I Believe We Are the Rapture Generation
ISBN: 9781973638872 • 298 pages • Westbow Press

BOOKS BY DR. ED KING

COOPERATING WITH YOUR DESTINY—Discovering God's Plan for Your Life

Seeking God's purpose for your life—what He put you on this planet to do—is the most important thing you could ever pursue! God has a good plan for your life that has been designed just for you. Your destiny is a partnership with God orchestrated to cause you to flourish and obtain your eternal reward—all you have to do is join with God's plan!
ISBN: 9781602731349 • 232 pages • Parsons Publishing House

DEDICATING YOUR HOUSE

Dedicating your house is a rite that every Christian should perform in order to live a quiet and peaceful life. Because you live in your house, you should want and expect God's blessings on it. One way to see those blessings is to thoughtfully and sacredly separate your house for the Lord's work and service. In this book, Dr. King lays out the biblical case for dedicating your house and provides eight easy-to-follow steps.
ISBN: 9781602730861 • 114 pages • Parsons Publishing House

THE TIMING OF GOD—His Timetable for Your Life

In this life–changing book, you will discover the true timetable that God has set up for you at creation. You will see everything in life has a time and a season. God wants to give you remarkable things to experience, but He wants to give them to you when you are ready to handle and enjoy them. After reading and studying this book, you will become more assured than ever that your next move will be by the inspiration and the timing of God.
ISBN: 978160273717 • 118 pages • Parsons Publishing House

BOOKS BY DR. ED KING

LOYALTY: GOING BEYOND FAITHFULNESS

Pastor Ed King elaborates on the distinctions between faithfulness and loyalty and focuses on lessons learned by looking at the brotherly love of Jonathan and David. Learn how God's grace will meet you to go past faithfulness and enter into loyalty. It all starts with a decision!
ISBN: 9781602730793 • 110 pages • Parsons Publishing House

WILL MY PET BE IN HEAVEN?

In this book, Pastor Ed King gives us a solid, biblical answer about your pet's afterlife. If you or someone you know has lost a pet, you will find great comfort and insight into what the Bible has to say about our beloved animals and their future in heaven.
ISBN: 9781602730687 • 92 pages • Parsons Publishing House

WHAT'S GOING ON?—Why I Believe We Are the Rapture Generation

Although the Bible tells us that no one knows the day or the hour of Jesus' return, God's Word does reveal solid information that illustrates how the signs of the times are lining up for His return to the earth. Pastor Ed King shares insight about the many signs appearing and circumstances playing out at this very hour.
ISBN: 9781973638872 • 298 pages • Westbow Press